Lexico

C000143080

Return items to **any** Swindon Library by closing
time on or before the date stamped. Only books
and Audio Books can be renewed - phone your
library or visit our website.

www.swindon.gov.uk/libraries

Central Library

01793 463238

20-12.13

CEN-7PIN

7/7/14

16.08.14

6 452 130 000

Copying recordings is illegal. All recorded items
are hired entirely at hirer's own risk

Swindon
BOROUGH COUNCIL

Also available from Continuum:

Corpus Linguistics: A Short Introduction
Wolfgang Teubert and Anna Čermáková

Words, Meaning and Vocabulary
An Introduction to Modern English Lexicology
Second Edition
Howard Jackson and Etienne Zé Amvela

Lexicology

A Short Introduction

M. A. K. Halliday and Colin Yallop

continuum

London ● New York

Continuum

The Tower Building	80 Maiden Lane
11 York Road	Suite 704
London	New York
SE1 7NX	NY 10038

First published in 2004 as part of *Lexicology and Corpus Linguistics*.

British Library Cataloguing-in-Publication Data
A catalogue record for this book is available from the British Library.

ISBN: HB: 0-8264-9478-1
     PB: 0-8264-9479-X

Library of Congress Cataloguing-in-Publication Data
A catalogue record for this book is available from the Library of Congress.

Typeset by YHT Ltd, London
Printed and bound in Great Britain by
Cromwell Press, Trowbridge, Wiltshire

Table of contents

1 Lexicology

M. A. K. Halliday

1.1 What is a word?

To many people the most obvious feature of a language is that it consists of words. If we write English, we recognize words on the page – they have a space on either side; we learn to spell them, play games with them like Scrabble, and look them up in dictionaries. It ought not to be difficult to know what a word is and how to describe it.

Yet when we look a little more closely, a word turns out to be far from the simple and obvious matter we imagine it to be. Even if we are literate English-speaking adults, we are often unsure where a word begins and ends. Is *English-speaking* one word or two? How do we decide about sequences like *lunchtime (lunch-time, lunch time), dinner-time, breakfast time*? How many words in *isn't, pick-me-up, CD*? Children who cannot yet read have little awareness of word boundaries, and often learn about them through word games, like 'I'm thinking of a word that rhymes with...'.

Even more problematic is whether two forms are, or are not, instances of the same word. Presumably if they sound alike but are spelled differently, like *horse* and *hoarse*, they are two different words. But how about pairs such as:

like 'similar to'	*like* 'be fond of'
part 'portion'	*part* 'to separate'
shape 'the outline of'	*shape* 'to mould'
content 'happy'	*content* 'that which is contained'

– not to mention *shape* as the old name for a kind of solid custard pudding?

We know that there is no single right answer to these questions, because different dictionaries take different decisions about what to do with them.

Then, what about variants like *take, takes, took, taking, taken*: are these five different words, or is there just one word *take* with many forms? Or *go, goes, went, going, gone*? Are *book* and *books, friend* and *friendly* one word or two? Are *big, bigger, biggest* three forms of a single word *big*? If so, what about *good, better, best*? Or *four* and *fourth, three* and *third, two* and *second*?

All these are problems within English, a language where the words are fairly clearly bounded. In Chinese it is much harder, because words are not marked off in writing; Chinese characters stand for **morphemes**, which are components of words. (For example, if English was written with Chinese characters, then a word like *free-dom* would be written with two characters, one for *free* and one for *dom*.) The Chinese are very conscious of morphemes, even before they are literate, because each one is pronounced as one syllable and hardly ever varies;

but they have much less intuition about what a word is. Many other writing systems, such as Japanese, Thai, Arabic and Hindi, also give no very consistent indication of word boundaries. When Ancient Greek was first written down, all the words were joined together without any spaces, and it was a few centuries before the word emerged as a clearly distinct unit.

So writing systems do not always identify words: partly because there are different kinds of writing system, but partly also because the languages themselves are different. There is no universal entity, found in every language, that we can equate with what in English is called a 'word'. And in unwritten languages the 'word' can be a very elusive thing.

Nevertheless there is a general concept underlying all this diversity; that is the **lexical item**. Every language has a **vocabulary**, or 'lexicon', which forms one part of its grammar – or, to use a more accurate term, one part of its **lexicogrammar**. The lexicogrammar of a language consists of a vast network of choices, through which the language construes its meanings: like the choices, in English, between 'positive' and 'negative', or 'singular' and 'plural', or 'past', 'present' and 'future'; or between 'always', 'sometimes' and 'never', or 'on top of' and 'underneath'; or between 'hot' and 'cold', or 'rain', 'snow' and 'hail', or 'walk' and 'run'. Some of these choices are very general, applying to almost everything we say: we always have to choose between positive and negative whenever we make a proposition or a proposal (*it's raining, it isn't raining*; *run! don't run!*). Others are very specific, belonging to just one domain of meaning; these arise only when we are concerned with that particular domain. The choice between rain and snow, for example, arises only if we are talking about the weather. Choices of this second kind are expressed as lexical items: e.g. *hot/ cold*; *rain/snow/hail*; *walk/run*.

3

If we are using the term 'word' to mean a unit of the written language, i.e. 'that which (in English) is written between two spaces', then ultimately all these choices are expressed as strings of words, or **wordings**, as in *it always snows on top of the mountain*. But teachers of English have customarily distinguished between **content words**, like *snow* and *mountain*, and **function words**, like *it* and *on* and *of* and *the*; and it is the notion of a content word that corresponds to our lexical item. Lexicology is the study of content words, or lexical items.

The example sentence in the last paragraph shows that the line between content words and function words is not a sharp one: rather, the two form a continuum or cline, and words like *always* and *top* lie somewhere along the middle of the cline. Thus there is no exact point where the lexicologist stops and the grammarian takes over; each one can readily enter into the territory of the other. So dictionaries traditionally deal with words like *the* and *and*, even though there is hardly anything to say about them in strictly lexicological terms, while grammars go on classifying words into smaller and smaller classes as far as they can go – again, with always diminishing returns.

This gives us yet a third sense of the term 'word', namely the element that is assigned to a **word class** ('part of speech') by the grammar. So the reason 'word' turns out to be such a complicated notion, even in English, is that we are trying to define it simultaneously in three different ways. For ordinary everyday discussion this does not matter; the three concepts do not in fact coincide, but they are near enough for most purposes. In studying language systematically, however, we do need to recognize the underlying principles, and keep these three senses apart. The reason our lexicogrammar is divided into 'grammar' and 'lexicology' (as in traditional foreign language textbooks, which had their section of the grammar and then a vocabulary added separately at the end) is because we need different models – different theories and techniques – for investigating these two kinds of phenomena, lexical items on the one hand and grammatical categories on the other. This is why **lexicology** forms a different sub-discipline within linguistics.

1.2 Methods in lexicology: the dictionary

There are two principal methods for describing words (now in our sense of **lexical items**), though the two can also be combined in various ways. One method is by writing a **dictionary**; the other is by writing a **thesaurus**.

The difference between a dictionary and a thesaurus is this. In a thesaurus, words that are similar in meaning are grouped together: so, for example, all the words that are species of fish, or all the words for the emotions, or all the words to do with building a house. In a dictionary, on the other hand, words are arranged simply where you can find them (in 'alphabetical order' in English); so the place where a word occurs tells you nothing about what it means. In the dictionary we find a sequence such as *gnome, gnu, go, goad*; and *parrot* is in between *parlour* and *parsley*.

In a dictionary, therefore, each entry stands by itself as an independent piece of work. There may be some cross-referencing to save repetition; but it plays only a relatively small part. Here are some typical entries from a fairly detailed dictionary of English, the two-volume *New Shorter Oxford English Dictionary*, 1993. (The full entries are much longer and omissions are indicated by ... in parentheses; the abridged entries given here serve to show the general structure and to illustrate the kind of detail included.)

bear /bɛ:/ *n.* [OE *bera* = MDu. *bere* (Du. *beer*), OHG *bero* (G *Bär*), f. Wgmc: rel. to ON *bjǫrn*.]

1. Any of several large heavily-built mammals constituting the family Ursidae (order Carnivora), with thick fur and a plantigrade gait. OE.

b With specifying wd: an animal resembling or (fancifully) likened to a bear. E17.

2. *Astron. the Bear* (more fully *the Great Bear*) = URSA *Major*; *the Lesser* or *Little Bear* = URSA *Minor*. LME.

3. *fig.* A rough, unmannerly or uncouth person. L16.

(. . .)

3. LD MACAULAY This great soldier . . . was no better than a Low Dutch bear.

(. . .)

Other phrases: **like a bear with a sore head** *colloq.* angry, ill-tempered.

(. . .)

bear /bɛ:/ *v.* Pa. t. **bore** /bɔ:/, (*arch.*) **bare** /bɛ:/. Pa.pple & ppl a. **borne** /bɔ:n/, BORN. See also YBORN. [OE *beran* = OS, OHG *beran*, ON *bera*, Goth. *bairan* f. Gmc f. IE base also of Skt *bharati*, Armenian *berem*, Gk *pherein*, L *ferre*.]

I *v.t.* Carry, hold, possess.

1 Carry (esp. something weighty), transport, bring or take by carrying; *fig.* have, possess. Now *literary* or *formal*. OE.

(. . .)

2 Carry about with or upon one, esp. visibly; show, display; be known or recognized by (a name, device, etc.); have (a character, reputation, value, etc.) attached to or associated with one. OE.

(. . .)

1 CHAUCER On his bak he bar . . . Anchises.

R. HOLINSHED This pope Leo . . . bare but seauen and thirtie yeeres of age.

SHAKES. *Macb.* I bear a charmed life, which must not yield To one of woman born.

E. WAUGH Music was borne in from the next room.

(. . .)

2 SHAKES. *Wint. T.* If I Had servants true about me that bare eyes To see alike mine honour as their profits.

STEELE Falshood . . . shall hereafter bear a blacker Aspect.

W. H. PRESCOTT Four beautiful girls, bearing the names of the principal goddesses.

A. P. STANLEY The staff like that still borne by Arab chiefs.

(. . .)

Phrases (. . .)

bear fruit *fig.* yield results, be productive. (. . .)

bear in mind not forget, keep in one's thoughts. (. . .)

cut /kʌt/ *v.* Infl. **-tt-**. Pa. t. & pple **cut.** See also CUT, CUTTED *ppl adjs.* ME [Rel. to Norw. *kutte*, Icel. *kuta* cut with a little knife, *kuti* little blunt knife. Prob. already in OE.]

I *v.t.* Penetrate or wound with a sharp-edged thing; make an incision in. ME.

b *fig.* Wound the feelings of (a person), hurt deeply.

(. . .)

1 N. MOSLEY The edge of the pipe cut his mouth, which bled. *fig.*: ADDISON Tormenting thought! it cuts into my soul.

b F. BURNEY He says something so painful that it cuts us to the soul.

(. . .)

Phrases: (. . .)

cut both ways have a good and bad effect; (of an argument) support both sides.

cut corners *fig.* scamp work, do nothing inessential. (. . .)

These entries are organized as follows:

1. the headword or **lemma**, often in bold or some other special font;
2. its pronunciation, in some form of alphabetic notation;
3. its word class ('part of speech');
4. its etymology (historical origin and derivation);
5. its definition;
6. citations (examples of its use).

Most dictionaries follow this general structure, but variations are of course found. For example, etymological information may come at the end of the entry rather than near the beginning. Let us look more closely at each item in turn.

1. The **lemma** is the base form under which the word is entered and assigned its place: typically, the 'stem', or simplest form (singular noun, present/infinitive verb, etc.). Other forms may not be entered if they are predictable (such as the plural *bears*, not given here); but the irregular past forms of the verbs are given (irregular in the sense that they do not follow the default pattern of adding *-ed*) and there is also an indication under *cut* that the *t* must be doubled in the spelling of inflected forms like *cutting*. An irregular form may appear as a separate lemma, with cross reference. This dictionary has such an entry for **borne** *v.* pa. pple & ppl a. of BEAR *v.*, indicating that *borne* is the past participle and participial adjective of the verb **bear**. In a language such as Russian, where the stem form of a word typically does not occur alone, a particular variant is chosen as lemma: nominative singular for nouns, infinitive for verbs, etc.

2. In most large and recent dictionaries, the pronunciation is indicated, as here, by the International Phonetic Alphabet in a broad, phonemic transcription. Some older dictionaries use a modified alphabet with a

keyword system, e.g. *i* as in 'machine', i as in 'hit', u as in 'hut'; and some dictionaries, especially those intended for use by children, simply use informal respellings, e.g. **emphasis** (EM-fa-sis) or **empirical** (em-PIR-ik-uhl).

3.   The word class will be one of the primary word classes (in English, usually verb, noun, adjective, adverb, pronoun, preposition, conjunction, determiner/article). To this class specification may be added some indication of a subclass – for example, count or mass noun, intransitive or transitive verb. The senses of the verbs illustrated here, for example, are identified as transitive verbs (*v.t.*). Some dictionaries, especially those compiled for learners of English, give more detailed word class information, showing, for example, the functional relations into which verbs can enter.

4.   The etymology may include, as here, not only the earliest known form and the language in which this occurs (e.g. Old English, OE for short) but also cognate forms in other languages. Some dictionaries may also include a suggested 'proto-' form, a form not found anywhere but reconstructed by the methods of historical linguistics; proto-forms are conventionally marked with an asterisk. The various forms of the noun *bear*, for example, suggest an ancestral form **ber-*, pre-dating the differentiation of languages such as Old English and Old High German. For many words, little or nothing is known of their history, and a common entry is 'origin unknown' (or the more traditional 'etym. dub.'!). This edition of the *Oxford* also indicates the first recorded use against each (sub)definition: OE means the word (or an earlier form of it) is attested in this sense in Old English texts, E17 means this sense is first recorded in the early seventeenth century, L16 that the sense is first recorded in the late sixteenth century.

5.   The definition takes one or both of two forms: description and synonymy. The description may obviously

need to include words that are 'harder' (less frequently used) than the lemmatized word. Some dictionaries, such as the *Longman Dictionary of Contemporary English* (first published in 1978), limit the vocabulary that they use in their descriptions. With synonymy, a word or little set of words of similar meaning is brought in, often giving slightly more specific senses. All definition is ultimately circular; but compilers try to avoid very small circles, such as defining *sad* as *sorrowful*, and then *sorrowful* as *sad*.

6. Citations, here grouped together under numbers referring back to definitions or senses, show how the word is used in context. They may illustrate a typical usage, or use in well-known literary texts, or the earliest recorded instances of the word. There may also be various 'fixed expressions' (idioms and clichés) and what the *Oxford* here calls 'phrases', where the expression functions like a single, composite lexical item (e.g. *bear fruit, bear in mind*).

The dictionary will usually use a number of abbreviations to indicate special features or special contexts – for example, *fig.* ('figurative'), *Astron.* ('Astronomy'), and so on. With a common word such as *bear* or *cut* there are likely to be subdivisions within the entry, corresponding to different meanings of the word.

Compound words, like *cutthroat* (as in *cutthroat competition*), and derivatives, like *cutting* (from a plant) or *uncut*, are often entered under the same lemma; in that case, compounds will appear under the first word (*cutthroat* under *cut*, *haircut* under *hair*), derivatives under the stem (both *cutting* and *uncut* under *cut*). But dictionaries adopt varying practices. In some dictionaries, compounds are given separate lemmata; and sometimes a derivational affix is used as lemma and derivatives grouped under that (for example, *antibody, anticlimax, antidote*, etc. all under *anti-*).

1.3 Methods in lexicology: the thesaurus

In a thesaurus, by contrast, there is no separate entry for each word. The word occurs simply as part of a list; and it is the place of a word in the whole construction of the book that tells you what it means.

Thus if we look for *cut* in Roget's *Thesaurus of English Words and Phrases* we will find it (among other places) in the middle of a paragraph as follows:

> **v. cultivate**; till (the soil); farm, garden; sow, plant; reap, mow, cut; manure, dress the ground, dig, delve, dibble, hoe, plough, plow, harrow, rake, weed, lap and top, force, transplant, thin out, bed out, prune, graft.

This may not seem to have very much organization in it; but it is actually the final layer in a comprehensive **lexical taxonomy**.

A lexical taxonomy is an organization of words into classes and sub-classes and sub-sub-classes (etc.); not on the basis of form but on the basis of meaning (that is, not grammatical classes but semantic classes). The principal semantic relationship involved is that of **hyponymy** (*x* is a hyponym of *y* means *x* 'is a kind of' *y*, e.g. *melon* is a hyponym of *fruit*). There is also another relationship, that of **meronymy** ('is a part of'), which may be used for classification. Such taxonomies are familiar in the language of everyday life, where they tend to be somewhat irregular and variable according to who is using them. Many of us might organize our shopping around taxonomies such as the one for *fruit* shown in Figure 1, perhaps according to how things are arranged in our local shop or market.

The taxonomies of living things on which biological science was founded in the eighteenth century are systematic variants of the same principle: the five kinds (classes) of *vertebrates* are *fishes*, *amphibia*, *reptiles*,

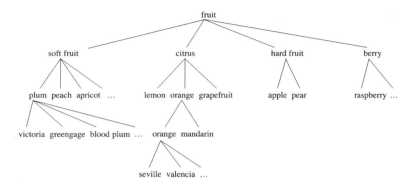

Figure 1 A partial taxonomy for fruit

birds and *mammals*; the eight kinds (orders) of *mammals* are *pachyderms, carnivores, cetaceans* ... Here each rank in the taxonomy is given a special name: *kingdom, phylum, class, order, family, genus, species, variety.*

A thesaurus takes all the lexical items that it contains and arranges them in a single comprehensive taxonomy. Roget's original *Thesaurus*, compiled over four decades from 1810 to 1850, was in fact conceived on the analogy of these scientific taxonomies; in his Introduction, Roget acknowledged his debt to Bishop John Wilkins, whose *Essay towards a Real Character and an Universal Language,* published in 1665, had presented an artificial language for organizing the whole of knowledge into an overarching taxonomic framework. Roget's taxonomy started with six primary classes: I, Abstract relations; II, Space; III, Matter; IV, Intellect; V, Volition; VI, Affections. Here is the path leading to one of the entries for the word *cut*. Starting from *Matter*, the path leads to *Organic* Matter, then to *Vitality* and *Special* Vitality (as opposed to Vitality in general); from there to *Agriculture*, then via the verb *cultivate* to the small sub-paragraph consisting of just the three words *reap, mow, cut*, which has no separate heading of its own. Thus there are eight ranks in the taxonomy, the last or **terminal** one being that of the lexical item itself. This path can be traced in the schematic representation shown in Figure 2.

Figure 2 is not how *cut* appears in the thesaurus of course; but we can reconstruct the path from the way the thesaurus is organized into chapters, sections and paragraphs. This particular example relates, obviously, only to one particular meaning of the word *cut*, namely cutting in the context of gardening and farming. But there is no limit on how many times the same word can occur; *cut* will be found in 26 different locations, each corresponding to a different context of use. There is an alphabetical index at the end of the book to show where each word can be found.

Thus a thesaurus presents information about words in a very different way from a dictionary. But although it does not give definitions, it provides other evidence for finding out the meaning of an unknown word. Suppose, for example, that you do not know the meaning of the word *cicuration*. You find that it occurs in a proportional set, as follows:

animal : vegetable
::   zoology : botany
:: cicuration : agriculture

The proportion shows that *cicuration* means 'animal husbandry'.

We cannot always construct such proportionalities. But the fact that a word is entered as one among a small set of related words also tells us a lot about what it means. Such a set of words may be closely synonymous, like *reap, mow, cut* – although not necessarily so; rather, they are **co-hyponyms**, or else **co-meronyms**, of some superordinate term. Thus *reap, mow, cut* (*cut* in this special sense) are co-hyponyms of *cut* in its more general sense; and the items in the next sub-paragraph (*manure*,

13

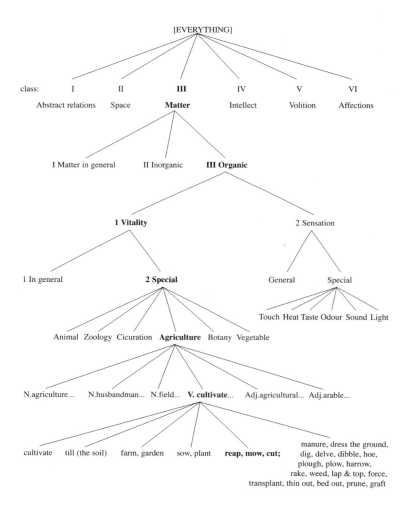

Figure 2 Schematic representation of a thesaurus entry. (Based on Roget's *Thesaurus of English Words and Phrases*, 1936)

dress the ground ... *prune, graft*) all represent stages in the cultivation process – that is, they are co-meronyms of *cultivate*. When we use a thesaurus to search for synonyms – as an aid to writing, for example – what we are really looking for are words that share a common privilege of occurrence; they do not ordinarily 'mean the same thing', but they share the same address, as it were, within our overall semantic space.

Another way of thinking about this shared privilege of occurrence that unites the words in one paragraph of the thesaurus is in terms of **collocation**. Collocation is the tendency of words to keep company with each other: like *fork* goes with *knife*, *lend* goes with *money*, *theatre* goes with *play*. Of course, if words do regularly collocate in this way, we shall expect to find some semantic relationship among them; but this may be quite complex and indirect. Collocation is a purely lexical relationship; that is, it is an association between one word and another, irrespective of what they mean. It can be defined quantitatively as the degree to which the probability of a word y occurring is increased by the presence of another word x. If you meet *injure*, you may expect to find *pain* somewhere around: given the presence of the word *injure*, the probability of the word *pain* occurring becomes higher than that determined by its overall frequency in the English language as a whole. The words that are grouped into the same paragraph in a thesaurus are typically words that have a strong collocational bond: either with each other or, more powerfully, each of them with some third party, some common associate that forms a network with them all.

1.4   History of lexicology: India, China, the Islamic world, Europe

When did lexicology begin? Like all systematic study of the **formal** patterns of language, lexicology depends on language being written down. Many oral cultures have developed highly elaborated theories of speech function and rhetoric; but it is only after writing evolves that attention comes to be focused on grammar and vocabulary. This typically began as a way of keeping alive ancient texts whose meanings were beginning to be lost as the language continued to change. In India as early as the third to second century BC, glossaries were drawn up to explain the difficult words in the Vedas, which by that time were already a thousand years old. These glossaries gradually evolved into what we would recognize today as dictionaries. In the seventh century AD, the scholar Amera Sinha prepared a Sanskrit dictionary, the *Amera Kosha*. More than ten centuries later this was still in use – it was translated into English by Colebrooke, and Colebrooke's translation, published in Serampur in 1808, is acknowledged by Roget as one source of ideas for his *Thesaurus*. Hamacandra's great dictionaries of Sanskrit and of Prakrit, the *Abhidhana Kintamani* and the *Desinamamala*, date from the twelfth century. By this time Indian scholarship in grammar and phonology had reached a high degree of sophistication, and dictionary-making took its place as part of the systematic description of language.

In China the earliest extant lexicological work is in fact a thesaurus, the *Er Ya* 'Treasury of Fine Words'. Compiled in this form in the third century BC, it is a list of about 3,500 words found in ancient texts, arranged under 19 headings: the first three sections contain words of a general nature – nouns, verbs and figurative expressions; the remaining 16 being topical groupings, headed Kin,

Buildings, Implements, Music, Sky (i.e. calendar and climate), Land, Hills, Mountains, Water (rivers and lakes), Plants, Trees, Insects and Reptiles, Fishes, Birds, Wild Animals and Domestic Animals. Each word is glossed, by a synonym or superordinate term, or else briefly defined. The Chinese paid little attention to grammar: since Chinese words are invariant, the question of why words change in form, which was what led the Indians, Greeks and Arabs to study grammar, simply did not arise. But their study of vocabulary developed in three directions: (1) recording dialect words, as in the *Fang Yan*, by Yang Xiong, in the first century BC; (2) investigating the origin of written characters, in *Shuo Wen Jie Zi*, by Xu Shen, in the first century AD; and (3) describing the sounds of words, classifying them according to rhyme, notably in the *Qie Yun* (AD 600) and *Tang Yun* (AD 750). By the time of the Ming and Qing dynasties, large-scale dictionaries and encyclopaedias were being compiled: notably the *Yongle Encyclopaedia* (1403–9) in 10,000 volumes, few of which, however, survive; and the *Kangxi Dictionary* (1716), containing some 50,000 characters together with their pronunciation and definition.

Both the Arabic and Hebrew traditions are rich in grammatical scholarship, and the earliest Arab grammarian, al-Khalil ibn Ahmed (died AD 791), is known to have begun work on an Arabic dictionary, using a phonological principle for ordering the words. But the leading lexicographers in the Islamic world were the Persians. The first dictionary of Farsi-dari, the Persian literary language, written by Abu-Hafs Soghdi in the ninth to tenth centuries, is now lost; but the eleventh-century *Lughat-e Fars* (Farsi dictionary), by Asadi Tusi, is extant. Persian scholars also produced bilingual dictionaries, Persian–Arabic (*Muqaddimat al-adab* 'Literary Expositor', by an eleventh-century scholar from Khwarezm,

Abul-Qasim Mohammad al-Zamakhshari) and, from the fifteenth century onwards, Persian–Turkish.

It is known that the Egyptians produced thesaurus-like topically arranged wordlists from as early as 1750 BC, although none has survived. In Greece, as in India, the earliest studies of words were glossaries on the ancient texts – Homeric texts, in the case of Greece. Apollonius, an Alexandrian grammarian of the first century BC, compiled a Homeric lexicon, but both this and the later glossaries by Hesychius are lost. Perhaps the greatest work of the Byzantine period was the *Suda*, a tenth-century etymological and explanatory dictionary of around 30,000 entries from literary works in Ancient, Hellenistic and Byzantine Greek and in Latin.

The development of dictionaries in the modern European context was associated with the spread of education and the promotion of emerging national literary languages. From about 1450 onwards bilingual dictionaries were being produced for use in schools, at first for learning Latin (Latin–German, Latin–English, etc.), but soon afterwards also for the modern languages of Europe. Many of the nation states of southern and eastern Europe then set up national academies, and these were responsible for establishing norms for the definition and usage of words: for example, the Italian *Vocabulario degli Academici della Crusca*, 1612; the *Dictionnaire de l'Académie française*, 1694 (the lexicographer Furetière was expelled from the Academy because he published his own dictionary, the *Universal Dictionary Containing All French Words*, in 1690 before the official one had appeared); the dictionary of the Spanish Academy in 1726–39, and that of the Russian Academy in 1789–94. By the nineteenth century the great publishing houses were bringing out extended series of lexicological works: notably in France (Littré, *Dictionnaire de la Langue française*, in four volumes plus supplement, in 1863–78; and Larousse,

Grand Dictionnaire Universel du XIXe siècle, an encyclopaedic dictionary in 15 volumes, 1865–76) and in
Germany (Meyer's *Great Encyclopaedic Lexicon* in 46
plus 6 supplementary volumes, 1840–55). Each of these
major works was followed by a large number of 'spin-off'
publications of various kinds.

1.5   Evolution of the dictionary and the thesaurus in England

As an illustration of how twentieth-century dictionaries
have evolved, we will take the example of English. But it
is important to bear in mind that English dictionaries did
not evolve in isolation from other traditions; they were
influenced from elsewhere in Europe and even from
further afield. Lexicography in England began in the form
of glossaries on 'difficult' words in manuscripts of Latin
texts: at first these were given in Latin, using simpler
words for the purpose, but by the seventh century they
were appearing in English (e.g. in the Épinal manuscript
preserved at a monastery in France). Next, such glosses
were taken out and arranged in a list (a 'glossary'); and
then various lists, especially of technical terms – for
example, in agriculture or in medicine – were collected
together into a 'vocabulary'. In the eighth and ninth
centuries compilers started arranging the words in
alphabetical order. By the thirteenth century the term
'dictionary' had come into use; the collections of words
were becoming considerably larger, and English–Latin
lists began to be compiled. The *Promptorium Parvulorum
sive Clericorum* 'Repository for Children and Clerics', by
Geoffrey 'the Grammarian' of Norfolk, dated about 1440,
contained some 12,000 words. It was during this century
that printing was introduced into Europe; the *Promptorium* was printed in 1499, and from then on the scope and

variety of published dictionaries grew rapidly. Sir Thomas Elyot's *Latin–English Dictionary* appeared in 1538; R. Howlet's *Abecedarium Anglico–Latinum* in 1552. Bilingual dictionaries of modern languages began with Palsgrave's English–French dictionary of 1530, and this was soon followed by dictionaries of English–Spanish and English–Italian. The arrangement of words by their strict alphabetical order had now become established practice; and lexicographers began introducing citations from literary works to illustrate usage in the foreign language.

The first monolingual English dictionary was published by Robert Cawdrey in 1604; this was *A Table Alphabeticall of Hard Usuall English Wordes*, which gave the spelling and meaning of about 2,500 terms. In 1616 John Bullokar's *An English Expositor* appeared, and in 1623 Henry Cockeram's *The English Dictionarie*. Cockeram's dictionary contained two parts: one of hard words, one of ordinary words, with words of each group being used to explain those of the other. The first dictionary which set out to include all words, and to define their meanings, was John Kersey's *A New English Dictionary* of 1702; shortly after this, in 1720, Nathan Bailey published his *Universal Etymological English Dictionary*, in which he added a new dimension to lexicography by including the history ('etymology') of each word. This work, along with other publications by Nathan Bailey, was the immediate precursor to Samuel Johnson's *Dictionary of the English Language*, which appeared in 1755. Dr Johnson's dictionary was a landmark not only in setting high professional standards in lexicography but also in establishing the role of the lexicographer as an authority on the 'correct' spelling, pronunciation and definition of words.

This normative function of a dictionary was a distinctive feature of two major American lexicographers of the first half of the nineteenth century, Noah Webster and Joseph Worcester. Webster in particular, in *An American Dictionary of the English Language* published in 1828, sought to codify American English as a distinct tongue, marked out by its own orthographic conventions; the modifications of spelling which he introduced in his dictionary, while much less radical than his original proposals, became accepted as the American standard.

In nineteenth-century lexicology in England, four achievements stand out.

1. One was Roget's *Thesaurus*, referred to earlier (1.3). Peter Mark Roget was a doctor who became a leading member of the Royal Society; his work of arranging the words and idiomatic phrases of the English language into one comprehensive semantic taxonomy occupied him for some 40 years. As already noted, he was influenced both by his predecessors in the Royal Society of 150 years earlier, in their construction of an artificial language for scientific taxonomy, and by the Indian tradition of lexicology that he knew from Colebrooke's translation of Amera Sinha's seventh-century Sanskrit dictionary.

2. Another was the *New English Dictionary on Historical Principles*, at first edited by James Murray and published in 12 volumes over the period 1884 to 1928 (by the Oxford University Press; hence its more familiar designation as *Oxford English Dictionary* or *OED*). This dictionary incorporated both extensive textual citations, a practice established in Charles Richardson's (1837) *New Dictionary of the English Language*, and detailed historical information about each word, following the principle established by Jacob and Wilhelm Grimm in their large-scale historical dictionary of German (begun in 1852, although not finally compiled and published until 1960). The *OED* contains over 400,000 entries and a little under two million citations. Four supplementary volumes appeared between 1933 and 1986, and a revised edition

of the entire dictionary was published in 1989 as *The Oxford English Dictionary*, second edition, in 20 volumes. The *Shorter*, *Concise* and *Pocket* Oxford dictionaries are all 'spin-offs' from this venture, and have been through numerous editions since the 1930s (one of which has been used for illustration in 1.2 above).

3. The third achievement was Joseph Wright's *English Dialect Dictionary*, published in six volumes in 1898–1905. This followed the tradition of dialect glossaries that had arisen earlier in various European countries, notably in Germany. Wright assigned each word to the localities where it was used, county by county; and detailed dialect surveys in the mid-twentieth century confirmed the comprehensiveness and accuracy of his lexicographical work.

4. Finally, the nineteenth-century dictionaries of the classical languages, Lewis and Short's *Latin–English Dictionary* and Liddell and Scott's *Greek–English Lexicon*, set a new standard that all subsequent bilingual dictionaries, classical or modern, have had to acknowledge.

In English-speaking countries in the twentieth century, dictionaries became a significant proportion of all publishing activity. In general the practices developed in nineteenth-century lexicography continued, but there was further expansion in three main areas: technical dictionaries, both monolingual and bilingual; learners' dictionaries, of English as a foreign or second language; and dictionaries of varieties of English other than those of England and America – principally Scots, Australian, Canadian, New Zealand and South African. In the latter part of the twentieth century, dictionaries of the so-called 'new varieties of English' also began to appear – for example, a *Dictionary of Jamaican English*, first published in 1967 and revised in 1980, and a *Dictionary of Caribbean English Usage*, 1996.

2 Words and meaning

Colin Yallop

2.1 Words in language

People sometimes play games with words. People may also recite or memorize lists of words – for example, when trying to learn the words of another language or to remember technical terms. And they may occasionally leaf through a dictionary looking at words more or less randomly. These are legitimate activities, enjoyable or useful as they may be. But they are not typical uses of words. Typically, human beings use words for their meaning, in context, as part of communicative discourse.

Vocabulary can be seen as part of lexicogrammar, a lexicogrammar that represents the choices which users of a language make, a lexicogrammar that represents our ability to *mean*. For, ultimately, language is about meaning. The main function of language – and hence of words used in language – is to mean.

This part of the book is particularly concerned with exploring the semantics of words. Section 2.2 offers some comments on meanings as presented in dictionaries. This is followed by brief discussion of potentially misleading notions about 'original meaning' (2.3) and 'correct meaning' (2.4). In 2.5 we try to explain what we mean by a social perspective on language and meaning, followed by some background on the theorizing of Saussure and Firth (2.6) and Chomsky and cognitive linguists (2.7). We then look at the implications of our theorizing for language and reality (section 2.8) and, to open up a multilingual perspective, we talk about the diversity of languages in the world (section 2.9) and about the process of translating from one language to another (2.10).

2.2 Words and meaning

A dictionary seems the obvious place to find a record of the meanings of words. In many parts of the English-speaking world, dictionaries have achieved such prestige that people can mention 'the dictionary' as one of their institutional texts, rather in the same way that they might refer to Shakespeare or the Bible. Such status means that a printed dictionary may easily be seen as the model of word-meanings. We may then, uncritically, assume that a dictionary in book form is the appropriate model of words as a component of language or of word-meanings stored as an inventory in the human brain or mind.

In fact a dictionary is a highly abstract construct. To do the job of presenting words more or less individually, in an accessible list, the dictionary takes words away from their common use in their customary settings. While this is in many respects a useful job, the listing of words as a set of isolated items can be highly misleading if used as a basis of theorizing about what words and their meanings are.

There is of course no such thing as 'the dictionary'. For a language such as English there are many dictionaries, published in various editions in various countries to suit various markets. The definitions or explanations of meaning in a dictionary have been drawn up by particular lexicographers and editors and are consequently subject to a number of limitations. Even with the benefit of access to corpora, to large quantities of text in electronic form, lexicographers cannot know the full usage of most words across a large community, and may tend to bring individual or even idiosyncratic perspectives to their work.

In the past, dictionaries were quite often obviously stamped by the perspective of an individual. Here is Samuel Johnson's definition of *patron*:

> **patron**, one who countenances, supports or protects. Commonly a wretch who supports with insolence and is paid with flattery.

Modern lexicographers generally aim to avoid this kind of tendentiousness. Certainly today's dictionaries tend to be promoted as useful or reliable rather than as personal or provocative. Nevertheless, despite the obvious drawbacks of a dictionary that represents an individual editor's view of the world, it is regrettable that dictionary users are not reminded more often of the extent to which dictionary definitions are distilled from discourse, and often from shifting, contentious discourse. In any event, lexicographers can never claim to give a complete and accurate record of meaning. A team of expert

25

lexicographers may by their very age and experience tend to overlook recent changes in meaning; or they may tend to write definitions which are elegant rather than accurate or simple; or they may follow conventions of definition which are just that – lexicographical conventions – rather than semantic principles.

Dictionaries often tend to favour certain kinds of technical identification, definitions that describe *dog* as *Canis familiaris*, or *vinegar* as 'dilute and impure acetic acid'. While this kind of information may sometimes be precisely what the dictionary-user is looking for, it is debatable whether it constitutes a realistic account of meaning. Many of us communicate easily and happily about many topics, including domestic animals, food, cooking, and so on, without knowing the zoological classification of animals or the chemical composition of things we keep in the kitchen. Perhaps people *ought* to know information like the technical names of animals or the chemical composition of things they buy and consume, whether as general knowledge or for their health or safety. But it would be a bold move, and a semantic distortion, to claim that people who don't know such information don't know the *meaning* of the words they use.

In general, it is unwise to assume that meaning is captured in dictionary entries, in the definitions or explanations given against the words. Dictionary definitions can and should be informative and helpful, and, when well written, they provide a paraphrase or explanation of meaning. But the meaning is not necessarily fully contained or exhaustively captured within such a definition. This is not to say that meanings are vague or ethereal. Within the conventions of a particular language, meanings contrast with each other in established and often precise ways. Speakers of the same language can convey meanings to each other with considerable precision. Words do not mean whatever we want them to mean, but are governed by social convention. Nonetheless, we cannot assume, without qualification, that the wording of a dictionary definition is an ideal representation of what a word means.

Extending this point, we normally use and respond to meanings in context. As users of language, we know that someone's mention of a recent television programme about big cats in Africa implies a different meaning of *cat* from a reference to the number of stray cats in the city of New York. And if someone talks about 'letting the cat out of the bag' or 'setting the cat among the pigeons', we know that the meaning has to be taken from the whole expression, not from a word-by-word reading of *Felis catus* jumping out of a bag or chasing *Columbidae*. Any good dictionary recognizes this by such strategies as listing different senses of a word, giving examples of usage, and treating certain combinations of words (such as idioms) as lexical units. But it is important to recognize that this contextualization of meaning is in the very nature of language and not some unfortunate deviation from an ideal situation in which every word of the language always makes exactly the same semantic contribution to any utterance or discourse.

For reasons such as these, we should be cautious about the view that words have a basic or core meaning, surrounded by peripheral or subsidiary meaning(s). For example, the very ordering of different definitions or senses in a dictionary may imply that the first sense is the most central or important. In fact there are several reasons for the sequence in which different senses are presented. Some dictionaries, especially modern ones intended for learners of the language, may use a corpus to establish which are the most frequent uses of a word in a large quantity of text, and may list senses of a word in order of frequency. Some lexicographers follow a historical order, giving the oldest recorded senses first (even if these are now obsolete and largely unknown). Or a compiler may order the senses in a way that makes the defining easier and more concise (which is probably of help to the reader, even though it intends no claim about the centrality of the first sense listed).

For instance, the word *season* is commonly used in phrases like *the football season*, *the rainy season*, *the tourist season*, *the silly season*, *a season ticket*, *in season*, *out of season*. These uses taken together probably outnumber what many people may think of as the fundamental meaning of *season* as 'one of the four seasons, spring, summer, autumn and winter'. But the lexicographer may judge it sensible to begin the entry with the 'four seasons of the year' sense, not only because this is perhaps what most readers expect, but also because the subsequent definitions of *season* as 'a period of the year marked by certain conditions' or 'a period of the year when a particular activity takes place', and so on, may seem easier to grasp if preceded by the supposedly basic sense.

To take another example, consider the first four senses listed for the noun *rose* in the *Macquarie Concise Dictionary* (1998). Some of the definitions have been abbreviated for this example:

> 1. any of the wild or cultivated, usually prickly-stemmed, showy-flowered shrubs constituting the genus *Rosa* ...
> 2. any of various related or similar plants.
> 3. the flower of any such shrubs ...
> 4. an ornament shaped like or suggesting a rose ...

The sequence of these senses is not random and the entry has been written or edited as a whole. The second sense, using the words 'related' and 'similar', assumes the reader has read the first definition; the third ('any such shrubs') presupposes the first and second; and so on.

The *Macquarie Concise* entry for *rose* also demon-strates that dictionaries are obliged to order items at more than one level. There are of course two quite distinct *roses*, the one we have just been talking about, and the one which is the past tense of *rise*. The *Macquarie* numbers these distinct meanings, as many dictionaries do, with a superscript [1] and [2], giving all the senses of the flower or bush (and the rose-like objects) under the first *rose*, and then simply indicating that the second *rose* is the past tense of *rise*. Probably most dictionary users find this the sensible order. Perhaps nouns seem more important, especially ones which have several different senses. Perhaps the second *rose* seems as though it is here accidentally – it really belongs under *rise*. Evidence from corpora suggests that the verb form *rose* (as in 'the sea level rose by 120 metres' or 'exports rose 2 per cent' or 'the evil genie rose from the jar') is used far more fre-quently than the noun; but this greater frequency does not seem to give priority to the verb in the minds of dictionary compilers and users.

It sometimes seems to be mere convention to list certain meanings first. Definitions of the word *have* often begin with the sense of 'possess' or 'own', and many people may indeed think of this as the fundamental or ordinary meaning of the word. In fact, corpus evidence indicates that the uses of *have* as an auxiliary verb (as in 'they have shown little interest') and in combinations like *have to* (as in 'we have to do better next time') are more frequent than uses like 'they have two cars' or 'we have a small house'.

Notions of what is a basic or central meaning of a word may thus be encouraged and perpetuated in a variety of ways, including common beliefs about words (which may or may not match actual usage) as well as lexicographical tradition. Sometimes such notions may be given formal recognition. For example, it is common to distinguish denotation from connotation. If taken as a serious semantic or philosophical claim, the distinction tends to separate what a word refers to from the associations that the word conjures up in the mind. More popularly, and sometimes simplistically, the distinction becomes a way of separating a core meaning from peripheral or variable aspects of meaning. But the distinction is by no means straightforward. It is complicated by the fact that what a word refers to in a particular context (as when talking to you I mention 'your cat') is not what is usually intended by *denotation* (which is more like 'any cat' or 'the class of cats'). The notion of denotation also runs the risk of identifying meaning with a class of objects or some idealized version thereof, as if meaning can be anchored in a world of concrete objects. This is clearly not very helpful in the case of many words, such as abstract nouns in general or verbs like *believe*, *dream*, *think*, *worry* or epithets like *good*, *kind*, *mysterious*, *poor*. And even where a denotation can be satisfactorily identified, it is not self-evident that this is an appropriate way of characterizing *meaning*.

The term *connotation* tends to slip awkwardly between something like 'peripheral meaning' and 'emotive meaning' and 'personal associations'. The notion of peripheral meaning simply raises the question of what is central or core meaning and why it should be so. It is clear from examples already given that the most frequently used sense of a word is not always the one that strikes most people as the core meaning. And it is equally clear that the older senses of a word are often neither the most frequent in current usage, nor the most basic by any other conceivable criterion.

Even 'emotive meaning', which might seem a good candidate for the margins of meaning, cannot always be considered peripheral. If I say to you 'Did you hear what happened to poor Sid?', the semantic contribution of *poor* must surely be 'emotive': the word says nothing about Sid's lack of wealth, but seeks to establish and elicit sympathy towards Sid. And this is hardly peripheral, since my question to you is most probably intended to introduce, and engage your interest in, a story of Sid's misfortune. Similar things can be said about the use of adjectives like *lucky* and *unfashionable*, which commonly serve to signal the speaker's attitude, and even about the verb *think* when used in utterances like 'I think the meeting starts at noon' (in which the words 'I think' serve to make the message less authoritative or dogmatic) or 'I think these are your keys' (as a polite way of telling someone they are about to leave their keys behind). Thus what might be termed 'emotive meaning' or 'attitudinal meaning' may sometimes be an integral part of discourse.

On the other hand, if 'associations' really are personal or idiosyncratic, then they hardly qualify as meaning at all, since they cannot contribute to regular meaningful exchanges. Suppose, for example, I have a fondness for a particular kind of flower, say, carnations, perhaps because of some valued childhood memory of them or other such personal experience. This may well have some consequences in my behaviour, including my discourse: I may often buy carnations, whereas you never do, I may mention carnations more than you do, and so on. But does it follow from any of this that you and I have a different meaning of the word *carnation*? Both of us, if we speak English, understand what is meant when someone says 'carnations are beautiful flowers', 'carnations are good value for money' and 'most people like carnations', whether we agree with the truth of these claims or not. Indeed, to *dis*agree with these statements requires an understanding of what they mean, just as much as agreeing with them does.

Of course to the extent that an association is shared throughout a community, it does contribute to discourse and becomes part of meaning. If a name like *Hitler* or *Stalin* is not only widely known but also widely associated with certain kinds of evil behaviour, then it becomes possible for people to say things like 'what a tragedy the country is being run by such a Hitler' or 'the new boss is a real Stalin'. And if people do say things like this, the names are on their way to becoming meaningful words of the language, along a similar path to that followed by words like *boycott* and *sandwich*, which had their origins in names of people associated with particular events or objects. (Note how *boycott* and *sandwich* are now written with initial lower-case letters rather than the capitals which would mark them as names. We might similarly expect to see the forms *hitler* and *stalin* appearing in print, if these names were to become genuine lexical items describing kinds of people.)

There may also be differences of experience and associations within a community which have systematic linguistic consequences. If, for example, some speakers of English love domestic cats while others detest them, this may well remain marginal to linguistic systems. But there may be small but regular linguistic differences between the speakers: for example, some people may always refer to a cat as 'he' or 'she' while for others a cat is always 'it', and some people may use *cat* as the actor of processes like *tell* and *think* (as in 'my cat tells me when it's time for bed' or 'the cat thinks this is the best room in the flat') whereas others would never use this kind of construction. To that extent we may have (slightly) different linguistic systems, say one in which a cat is quasi-human in contrast to one in which a cat is firmly non-human. In that case, it is legitimate to recognize two somewhat different meanings of *cat* and two minor variants of English lexicogrammar.

For meaning is ultimately shaped and determined by communal usage. A dictionary definition of a word's meaning has authority only in so far as it reflects the way in which those who speak and write the language use that word in genuine communication. In this sense, meaning has a social quality, and while it is sometimes convenient to think of the meaning of a word as a concept, as 'something stored in the human mind', this is legitimate only to the extent that the concept is seen as an abstraction out of observable social behaviour.

An overview of issues to do with word meaning, and references to classic discussions such as Lyons (1977), can be found in the first two sections of Chapter 3 of Jackson and Ze Amvela (1999). We will return to the issues in the following sections of this chapter, both to elaborate our own views of language as social behaviour and of meaning as a social phenomenon, and to contrast our views with others.

2.3 Etymology

In this section we look briefly at the relevance of historical development. Changes in language – specifically changes in meaning – are inevitable, but they are sometimes decried, as if language ought to be fixed at some period in time. In fact, attempts to fix meanings or to tie words to their 'original' meanings deny the social reality of linguistic usage. (In the following section, 2.4, we will look more generally at attempts to prescribe and regulate meaning.)

Warburg tells the story of a lawyer who disputed a witness's use of the word *hysterical* (Warburg 1968, pp. 351–2). The witness had described a young man's condition as 'hysterical'. But, the lawyer pointed out, this word was derived from the Greek *hystera*, meaning 'uterus' or 'womb'. The young man didn't have a uterus, so he couldn't possibly be 'hysterical'.

Would a good lawyer really expect to score a point

by this kind of appeal to etymology? Few of us are likely to be persuaded to change our view of the current meaning of the word *hysterical*. It is true that the word is based on the Greek for 'uterus' (and the Greek element appears in that sense in English medical terms such as *hysterectomy* and *hysteroscopy*). But it is also true that words may change their meaning and that the modern meaning of *hysterical* has more to do with uncontrolled emotional behaviour, by men or women, than with the uterus as a bodily organ.

Sometimes an older sense of a word survives in limited contexts, while the most frequent meaning has changed. The word *meat*, for example, now has the common meaning of 'animal flesh used as food', but its Old English antecedent was a word that had the more general meaning of 'food'. Traces of the older more general meaning can be seen in phrases and sayings like *meat and drink* (i.e. 'food and drink') and *one man's meat is another man's poison* (i.e. 'one man's food is another man's poison'). The word *sweetmeat* also demonstrates the older sense. Other than in these restricted contexts, the older meaning of the word has become not only obsolete but also irrelevant to modern usage. If you ask today whether a certain supermarket sells meat, or talk about the amount of meat consumed in Western Europe, or have an argument about what kind of meat is in a meat pie, no one who speaks English pauses to wonder whether you really intend *meat* to mean 'food in general' rather than 'animal flesh'.

Indeed, older meanings become lost from view, and phrases and sayings may even be reinterpreted to suit the new meaning. The word *silly* had an older sense of 'happy' (compare German *selig*, 'blessed') but this sense has been ousted by the current meaning of 'foolish' or 'absurd'. A phrase sometimes applied to the county of Suffolk in eastern England, *silly Suffolk*, dates from the days when Suffolk was one of the wealthier counties, and therefore 'happy' or 'fortunate'. But if the saying is quoted at all these days, either it has to be explained, as we have just done here, or it is taken to be an allegation of foolishness or backwardness.

The word *prove* once had the sense of 'try' or 'test' but the most common modern meanings are of course 'show beyond doubt' (as in 'we all suspect him of corruption but no one has been able to prove it') and 'turn out' (as in 'the book proved to have lots of useful information in it'). The saying that *the exception proves the rule* shows the older sense – an exception indeed 'tests' whether a rule is really valid or needs to be reformulated. But the saying is often reinterpreted, with *prove* taken in its modern sense, to mean that an odd exception actually confirms a rule. This is clearly not true – an exception doesn't support a rule, it challenges it – but such is the power of current meaning to efface the old.

There is a long history of interest in etymology, in 'where words have come from', and many large dictionaries of English include etymological information (see McArthur 1992, pp. 384–6, Landau 1989, pp. 98–104, Green 1996, esp. pp. 337–48). Unfortunately, until the development of methodical historical linguistics in the nineteenth century, much etymology was highly speculative and often erroneous. Misguided guesswork about the origins of words can be found in ancient Europe – for example, in the work of Varro, a Roman grammarian active in the first century BC (Green 1996, p. 41) – and the practice of trying to relate as many words as possible to a relatively small number of allegedly simple or basic words was common until the mid-nineteenth century. Green cites a classic example from the late eighteenth century, in which a whole array of English words were claimed to be derived from or based on the word *bar*: thus a *bar* is a kind of defence or strengthening, and a *barn* is a covered enclosure to protect or defend what is stored in it, a *barge* is a strong boat, the *bark* of a tree is its protection, the *bark* of a dog is its defence, and so on (Green 1996, p. 353). In fact, careful historical research indicates that the word *bar*, as in the bars in a fence or across a window, came into English from Old French, while *barn* is from an Old English compound meaning 'barley store', *barge* is related to an Old French word for a kind of boat, the *bark* of a tree is a word of Scandinavian origin, and the *bark* of a dog goes back to the Old English verb *beorcan*, 'to bark', which is not related to the other *bark*. These various words are of different origins, there is no evidence that they are all based on *bar*, and the idea that they are all clustered around the notion of defence is pure speculation.

Occasionally, an erroneous origin has become enshrined in the language by a process of 'folk etymology', in which the pronunciation or spelling of a word is modified on a false analogy. The word *bridegroom*, for example, has no historical connection with the *groom* employed to tend horses. The Old English antecedent of *bridegroom* is *brydguma*, where *guma* is a word for 'man'. The word ought to have become *bridegoom* in modern English, but as the word *guma* fell out of use, the form *goom* was popularly reinterpreted (with a change in pronunciation and spelling) as *groom*. A similar process of trying to make the odd seem familiar sometimes applies to words adapted from other languages. The *woodchuck*, or 'ground hog', has a name taken from a North American Algonquian word which, in its nearest anglicized pronunciation, might be something like *otchek* or *odjik*. The word has nothing to do with either *wood* or *chuck*, but was adapted to seem as if it did.

There is nothing wrong with being interested in where a word has come from, and many people who use modern dictionaries expect historical or etymological information to be included. For much of the nineteenth and twentieth centuries, most dictionaries gave considerable prominence to historical information. The first complete edition of what is now commonly referred to as the 'Oxford dictionary' was entitled *A New English Dictionary on Historical Principles*, and it set out to record the history of words, not just their current meanings (see 1.5 above; but not all subsequent Oxford dictionaries, including various abridged editions and dictionaries for learners, have had the same historical priority). It hardly needs to be said that modern professional lexicographers try to avoid speculation and guesswork and to give only information based on good research.

It is indeed often interesting to know something of a word's history and its cognates in other languages, and many (though not all) modern dictionaries still include etymological information. English happens to share with most European languages a reasonably well-documented Indo-European heritage. Languages like Greek, Latin and Sanskrit, as well as a 'proto-Germanic' language ancestral to modern English, German and other Germanic languages, can be shown to be historically related within an Indo-European 'family' of languages. The entry for *bear* (in the sense of 'carry') in the *New Shorter Oxford*, as cited earlier in 1.2, illustrates the way in which some dictionaries list cognates: the etymology includes not only forms considered to be ancestral to the modern English, in this case Old English *beran*, but also forms from other Germanic languages which are parallel to Old English rather than ancestral to it, such as Old Norse *bera* and Gothic *bairan*. The *Oxford* also lists forms that are parallel to Germanic, including Sanskrit *bharati*, Greek *pherein* and Latin *ferre*. As the *Oxford* entry implies, linguists hypothesize that there was an Indo-European form from which the Sanskrit, Greek, Latin and Proto-Germanic forms were separately derived.

Sometimes there have been intriguing changes of meaning. The word *town*, for example, can be traced back to an Old English form *tun* (with a long vowel, pronounced something like modern English *oo* in *soon*). We can connect this form with related words in other modern Germanic languages, notably *tuin* in Dutch and *Zaun* in German. There are regular patterns of sound change which (partly) explain how the forms have become different: modern English *out*, *house*, *mouse*, all pronounced with the same diphthong as in *town*, can be related to Old English *ut*, *hus*, *mus* (all with a long *u*) as well as to Dutch *uit*, *huis*, *muis* and German *aus*, *Haus*, *Maus*. But in the case of the forms related to *town*, Dutch *tuin* means not 'town' but 'garden' and German *Zaun* means neither 'town' nor 'garden' but 'fence'. There was also a similar word in Celtic languages, namely *dun*, meaning something like 'citadel' or 'fortified town'. This element is evident in some Roman place names incorporating Celtic elements, like *Lugdunum*, modern *Lyons*, and in names such as *Dunedin*, an old Celtic name now generally replaced in Scotland by the anglicized form *Edinburgh*, but still the name of a city in New Zealand. Thus the word must once have referred to fortified settlements. By modern times the English word *town* has generalized in meaning to refer to any substantial urban centre (between a village and a city in size and importance) while the Dutch word *tuin* has come to mean 'enclosed cultivated land', that is 'a garden', rather than an enclosed town, and the German *Zaun* has narrowed to the enclosure itself, or 'fence'.

Such information is not only interesting to many readers, but it is also often valuable as an accompaniment to historical and cultural research. Moreover, modern European languages not only have a certain shared heritage, but they have also continued to draw on it in various ways. Latin words can still be found in uses as diverse as the English translation of Freud (the *ego* and the *id*) and the mottoes of army regiments (such as *Ubique*, 'everywhere', the motto of the British Royal Artillery). Some Latin phrases are indeed everywhere, even if no longer fully understood. Notable examples are *etc.*, the abbreviated form of *et cetera*, 'and the rest'; *e.g.*, short for *exempli gratia*, 'for (the sake of) example'; and *a.m.* and *p.m.* (*ante meridiem*, *post meridiem*). Latin has been regularly used in anatomical description (*levator labii superior*, the 'upper lip raiser' muscle, or *corpus callosum*, the 'callous (hard) body' in the brain), and in botany and zoology (*quercus*, 'oak', for a genus of trees, or *felis*, 'cat', for the genus of animals that includes domestic cats and some closely related species). Latin phrases such as *de facto*, *in camera*, *sine die*, *sub judice* and *ultra vires* are known in legal contexts, and some of them have a wider currency (such as the Australian use, even outside legal contexts, of the phrase 'a de facto' to mean 'a common-law spouse').

Greek and Latin have also provided a rich source of modern coinage. Words like *altimeter*, *electroencephalogram*, *hydrophone* and *telespectroscope* are obviously not themselves classical words: they have been built from Latin and Greek elements to deal with relatively recent technological innovation. Indeed, it has become so customary to use such elements as building blocks, that Latin and Greek are often combined in hybrid forms, as in Greek *tele-* with Latin *vision*, or Latin *appendic-* with Greek *-itis*.

But it is by no means just new items of technology, like cardiographs and synthesizers, that attract classical naming. Greek and Latin elements are integral to our standardized systems of calculating and measuring (*centigrade*, *centimetre*, *kilogram*, *millisecond*, *quadrillion*). Concepts like *social security*, *multimedia*, *globalization* and *privatization*, though essentially twentieth-century concepts, are conceived in classical forms. A classical heritage similarly underlies terms like *interdisciplinarity* (which I heard used at Macquarie University in discussions about creating links among different academic 'disciplines' or areas of learning) and *interdiscursivity* (which I have seen on a whiteboard in a university lecture theatre but not yet understood). And terms formed with Greek and Latin elements like *intra, non, post, pseudo, ultra* are used as much in administration or business or politics as in science or technology (*intrastate, noncompliance, postdated, pseudo-solution, ultraconservative*).

Nevertheless, as we have already argued, the history of a word is not the determinant of its current meaning, and the greatest persisting drawback of etymological studies is that they may be misused to support assertions about what words 'ought' to mean. No modern dictionary (including Oxford's *New English Dictionary*) seriously misuses historical information in this way. And, for the greater part of English vocabulary, no one seriously proposes that an older meaning of a word is the only correct meaning. But where a shift in meaning is relatively recent, and particularly where a newer sense of a word is evidently competing with an older sense, some people may deplore the change and attempt to resist it. Thus in the seventeenth century, the English word *decimate* was used to mean something like 'take or remove one tenth from', as in 'tithing', that is taxing people one-tenth of their income or property, or in the sense of killing one in ten. (Executing one in ten of a group of soldiers was a punishment sometimes used in the ancient Roman empire.) Nowadays the word is most commonly used to mean 'destroy most of', as if the 'decimation' now means reducing to one-tenth, rather than reducing to nine-tenths. Some people, especially those who have had a classical education and are aware of the ancient Roman punishment, condemn the modern usage as loose and unwarranted.

Whatever our feelings about respecting tradition or preserving history, it has to be said that such attempts to resist changes in general usage are rarely, if ever, successful. What usually happens is that by the time a shift is in progress, a majority accepts or doesn't notice the change, and only a minority condemns or resists the change. At this point, the minority may claim that their usage is educated or correct, and that the majority usage is careless or mistaken. But the minority usage is at risk of seeming unduly conservative and pedantic, and the situation is usually resolved by the disappearance of the minority usage. Over the years, people have deplored the changes in meaning of words like *arrive, deprecate* and *obnoxious* and have been able to argue that the older meaning was more faithful to the etymology. Thus *arrive* used to mean 'to reach a shore' rather than to reach anywhere (and the older meaning could be justified by appeal to the French *rive* 'shore, riverbank'); *deprecate* once meant 'to pray against, pray for deliverance from' rather than the modern 'to disapprove of, criticize' (and this too could be justified etymologically, given the Latin *deprecatus* 'prayed against'); and *obnoxious* meant 'liable to criticism or punishment' (Latin *obnoxius* 'exposed to harm'), whereas the modern meaning is 'unpleasant, offensive'. Needless to say, the older meanings are now virtually unknown – except to those who find them in dictionaries and other records of the past.

Finally, we should note the need to be cautious about the idea of 'original meaning'. Sometimes we can identify the origin of a word – as, for instance, with the word *boycott*, which is believed to have come from the name of a land agent in nineteenth-century Ireland, who was 'boycotted' by tenants. But in many cases, there is no justification for calling an earlier meaning 'original'. The most common current meaning of *nice* – pleasant or enjoyable – has probably come from an earlier meaning,

41

something like 'delicate' or 'dainty'. But this meaning can scarcely be called original. It probably came from earlier use of the word to mean 'finely differentiated' or 'requiring care and discrimination' (compare a traditional legal phrase 'a nice point'), which must in turn have come from the Latin *nescius* 'ignorant'. But even the Latin word and its meaning are only original relative to modern English. Latin is also a language with a history. It descended from something spoken previously, just as much as modern Italian came from Latin or modern English from Old English. In short, however interesting and instructive the past may be, not all of it is accessible to us and not all of it is relevant. The past is not the present, nor is the history of a word its meaning.

2.4 Prescription

The idea which we have been looking at in the previous section, that a word ought to mean what it used to mean, is just one instance of what can be called a prescriptive approach to language. More generally, there have been many and various attempts to prescribe how language ought to be – prescriptions about pronunciation, for example, or rules about correct grammar, as well as claims about the proper meanings of words. Many of these attempts have been misguided if not perverse, and it became axiomatic in twentieth-century linguistics to reject prescriptivism. A common slogan of linguists was that 'linguistics is descriptive, not prescriptive'.

As a commitment to scientific method and ethical research, the slogan is exemplary. Whether investigating the physiology of speech production, recording what people say to each other in specific situations or examining the frequencies of words in printed texts, linguists, like all scholars and researchers, are under obligation to describe what they find. Even allowing that complete objectivity is unattainable, and that there will always be controversy about what exactly constitutes 'describing what you find', there is an indisputable obligation to aim to describe what is there, rather than to describe what you would like to be there or what you think ought to be there.

The slogan also represents a justifiable reaction to some of the prescriptivism of the past. In seventeenth- and eighteenth-century Europe, for example, some scholars and writers believed that it was necessary to regulate language and to set up academies for this purpose, such as the Académie Française, founded in 1634 and charged with compiling a French dictionary and with ruling on matters of grammar, vocabulary and usage. Though no academy was ever set up in Britain, there were certainly calls to refine and reform the English language. To some extent, these ambitions were motivated by a desire for regularity and consistency. Since it is important both to understand the weakness of prescriptive approaches to language and to recognize the genuine normativity inherent in language, we will consider two examples in some detail, first the history of comparative forms like *(more) bigger*, and second the proposal that prepositions shouldn't end sentences.

In English grammar, by the seventeenth century, the old pattern of forming comparative and superlative adjectives by endings (as in *big, bigger, biggest* or *tall, taller, tallest*) had begun to blend with a newer pattern using the words *more* and *most* (as in *evil, more evil, most evil* or *corrupt, more corrupt, most corrupt*). In Shakespeare's writings, for example, we can find the two patterns combined, as in *more better, more corrupter, most unkindest, most coldest*. But eighteenth-century grammarians began to criticize this practice, apparently on the grounds that only one of the two devices (either the ending or the *more/most*) is logically necessary to convey the meaning. Modern English usage has been partly influenced by these grammatical strictures. People nowadays quite often say things like *more kinder* or *most earliest*, but they tend to avoid them in writing, and editors are likely to delete the *more* or *most*. Written usage is still not exactly regular, however, since the tendency is to use the endings on monosyllabic words (*colder, coldest, higher, highest, later, latest*) and to use *more* and *most* with polysyllabic words (*more difficult, more interesting, most intelligent, most troublesome*). But this is only a generalization: some monosyllabic words do take *more* (*more tired*, for instance) and for some words of two syllables it seems perfectly acceptable to go either way (*shallower* or *more shallow, commonest* or *most common*). There are also the 'irregular' forms *better, best, worse, worst*. (For an overview of usage see Biber *et al.* 1999, pp. 521–5, and for details of past as well as more modern usage, see Fries 1940, pp. 96–101.)

Despite some variation in usage, forms such as *more bigger* and *most highest* are usually disapproved of by editors and teachers. While there may be a superficial appeal in simplifying such phrases to the single words *bigger* and *highest*, there are two difficulties to be noted. The first is that users of language will rarely, if ever, be bound by the dictates of individuals and academies, however educated or well informed those authorities may be. Many speakers of English continue to say things like *more kinder* and *most earliest*, even after they have been told not to. And imagine the reaction (or indifference) of the community at large if linguists or teachers were to recommend that we regularize the language by saying *gooder* and *goodest* rather than *better* or *best*, or *badder* and *baddest* rather than *worse* and *worst*. Whatever arguments might be put forward, that forms like *gooder* are simpler, more regular or more logical than what we actually say, most people would continue to follow their customary practice and would consider the recommendation absurd. With few exceptions, language does not change because of regulation, it changes according to its own communal patterns.

The second problem in making language more logical or regular is that it is not at all self-evident what constitutes logic or regularity in linguistic matters. It is somewhat clearer, and rather more carefully discussed, what logic means in thinking and reasoning, or what regularity means in the study of natural phenomena. But linguistic systems generate their own logics and regularities. Is it really illogical to say *more kinder*? If it is the redundancy that is illogical, then by similar argument, we might claim, for example, that plural forms are redundant and illogical after numerals. A numeral already signals that the noun must be understood as plural, and we could therefore write *five dollar, a hundred student, a thousand spectator*. (And some languages, such as Welsh, do indeed use the singular form of a noun after a numeral.) In fact if we look dispassionately at the patterns of languages, we find a variety of ways of organizing the lexicogrammar to express meaning, and it is not at all obvious why any of them should be regarded as more or less logical than others. Is it more logical for adjectives to precede nouns (as they mostly do in English, German or Japanese) or to follow nouns (as they mostly do in French, Italian or Indonesian)? Is there any reason why we should express contrasting verb meanings by suffixes (as English does with, say, *walk, walked, chase, chased*) rather than by auxiliary verbs (as English does with, say, *will walk, might walk, will chase, might chase*)? Is it neater or more regular to signal meanings like 'for', 'in' and 'on' by separate words preceding a noun (as English and most European languages do) or by suffixes on the noun (as languages as diverse as Finnish, Turkish and Australian Aboriginal languages mostly do)? What is logical and regular is the

45

way in which each language underlies the linguistic behaviour of its speakers, the way in which each language builds a system out of its systems. The positioning of adjectives, the mechanics of the verb system, the use of prepositions or noun suffixes are not just trivial and isolated features of a language but are woven together in a complex, coherent and powerful lexicogrammar.

To return to the point about attempts to reform English, our second example is a rule sometimes imposed on English that sentences should not end with prepositions. According to the severest version of this rule, prepositions belong before a noun or pronoun, as in *for Uncle Leo, for me, in Singapore, in the afternoon, on Fridays, on the table.* A sentence in which a preposition appears other than before a noun or pronoun, like 'that's the book which I've been looking for', should be rephrased as 'that's the book for which I've been looking'; and a question like 'what is she looking at?' should be rephrased as 'at what is she looking?' This rule seems to have been invented by Dryden in the seventeenth century (Strang 1970, p. 143) and since then it has been often promoted, possibly beyond Dryden's intentions, and widely ignored or ridiculed.

In modern grammars, a preposition such as the 'for' in 'what are you looking for?' is sometimes said to be 'stranded' (see, e.g., Biber *et al.* 1999, pp. 105–8). The reasons for wanting to avoid 'stranded' prepositions probably include the fact that prepositions do not occur at the end of sentences in Latin (and Latin has often been held up as a model which other languages should conform to) and the very name *preposition*, which might seem, etymologically, to imply that these words should always be 'pre-posed' before another word.

But Latin grammar is not the same as modern English grammar, and the etymology of the name *preposition* does not impose any requirement on well-established

English usage (any more than *premises* must mean '(things) sent beforehand' or *prevent* must mean 'come before'). While many writers, having been schooled in Dryden's rule, may now prefer to avoid sentence-final prepositions in formal English, most of us continue to ask questions like 'what were you looking for?' and 'who did you give it to?', and find the rephrased versions awkward or pompous. Indeed, the strength of communal resistance to arbitrary regulation is seen in the way in which the rule is mocked by pronouncements such as 'a preposition is a bad word to end a sentence with' or the witticism ascribed to Winston Churchill 'this is a form of pedantry up with which I will not put'.

While it may sometimes seem desirable to make language more logical or consistent, the fundamental challenge to regulators is that the patterns of language emerge as a matter of social convention. Regularity and consistency are important factors in this process, but not the only ones or the pre-eminent ones. As we have already suggested, the complexity of language and its processes of acquisition and change are such that it is not always clear what exactly logic and consistency mean in linguistic practice. If *most coldest* ought to be simplified or regularized, should it be to *coldest* or to *most cold*? And if this reform is important, why is it not equally important to get rid of redundant plural forms after numerals or to tidy up the English verb system? Why not get rid of the irregular and redundant word *am*, and simplify *I am* to *I are*, on the analogy of *you are* and *we are*? (We already say *aren't I?* rather than *amn't I?* which takes us some of the way towards this regularization.) Why not make all verbs regular, replacing *ran* with *runned*, *wrote* with *writed*, and so on? The absurdity of trying to impose some externally conceived general notion of logic and simplicity on language puts a harsh spotlight on the odd details that are on reformist agendas.

Indeed, many people have tried to reform or regularize a language or to stop it from changing, but few have had much success. In general, languages change as societies and cultures do: as we differ from our grandparents, whether radically or not, in our beliefs, our perspectives, our social behaviour, our hobbies, our dress, so we differ from them, significantly or trivially, in our accent, in our idiom, in the words we use and the meanings we exploit. Changes in language do not happen uniformly across the world, and perhaps not even at a constant rate – there may be periods of rapid change and periods of relative stability. But change is observable, everywhere where the history of languages can be studied.

We should nevertheless be clear that an argument against regulation and prescription is not an argument against normativity in principle. The social nature of language brings a normativity of its own. As children we learn our linguistic patterns in the community in which we function, from our peers and from the adults with whom we interact. We learn the conventions of the written language which our community has inherited. And the patterns and conventions that underlie linguistic behaviour around us exert a strong pressure to conform: as human beings we are powerfully motivated, not only to understand and be understood, but also to belong.

As we enter places of formal education and employment, we may be subject to specific linguistic norms, the kinds of norms that govern the writing of university essays or press releases or product information or government reports. Here we may well be in relatively circumscribed domains, where norms may be imposed more directly and more authoritatively. Thus a commercial company may have rules about the structure and wording of the memorandums written by its employees, a journal may have requirements about the style and presentation of papers which it is prepared to publish, a government department may follow conventional guidelines about the format and style of its documentation, and so on. (For more discussion of 'controlled' language, especially nomenclatures, see 2.8 below.)

It is in such domains that arbitrary prescriptions of the kind that tell us to write *shallower*, not *more shallow*, or to avoid ending sentences with prepositions, may have some measure of success. To some extent, arbitrary rulings in well-defined contexts are necessary, simply to yield consistency in, for example, the way in which dates are written or bibliographies compiled or reports presented. Hopefully the focus of those who write the relevant style guides or otherwise determine conventions in such settings is on clarity and consistency and efficiency, and on meaningful rather than empty traditions.

Moreover, even in society at large, it is important, even essentially human, to bring moral perspectives to bear on social and cultural changes. Social and cultural changes can, and should be, evaluated for their effects on human well-being, on the distribution of resources, on fairness and justice, difficult and contentious though the processes and criteria of evaluation may be. And to the extent that language reflects and supports behaviour and social structures, it is open to moral evaluation. Without such evaluation there would be no debate about sexism and racism in language, no possibility for argument about clarity and truth in language. Thus most of us do accept style guides that promote inclusive or egalitarian language, guidelines that provide for a certain degree of consistency of format in journals and bibliographies, courses that teach report writing, and so on.

The argument against prescription is not an argument against normativity in principle. But linguistic norms must be founded in social agreement on issues that matter to people – in a recognition by most people that we ought to eliminate racist words from the language, or that it is worth some effort to make instruction manuals as clear as possible, or that bibliographies are much easier to use if they follow standard conventions. This kind of commitment does not constitute justification for prescriptions about whether you can end a sentence with a preposition, and it gives no support to rulings based on individual interpretations of what might make language more regular, nor to arguments that language should be fixed once and for all in some supposedly golden age.

2.5 A social view of language and meaning

In this book we take the view that language is social behaviour and meaning a social phenomenon. By this we mean that language is more than an individual possession or ability, that language 'exists' because of its life in social interaction, that meaning is shaped and negotiated in social interaction and that meaning must be studied with due recognition of its social setting.

The concept of meaning itself is difficult to define and it is no exaggeration to say that modern linguistics has failed to formulate a widely agreed theory of meaning. But the fact that there is something elusive and mysterious about meaning need not embarrass us, any more than humans should be embarrassed by the difficulty of understanding and defining exactly what we mean by time, number, life and other fundamental concepts of our existence. Most of us readily acknowledge that we cannot give a snappy definition of what time is, but we are still conscious of what we call the passing of time, we know the difference between yesterday and tomorrow, we even make it possible for ourselves to measure and quantify time by counting the alternations of daylight and darkness, constructing a twenty-four-hour day, and so on. Similarly, it is hard to give a technical definition of life. Dictionaries resort to phrases like 'the state of being alive' or to descriptions of what distinguishes living beings from dead ones or living beings from inanimate objects. In so doing they demonstrate both the difficulty of what they are trying to do and the good sense of drawing on our experience: we know that some things (people, animals, plants) live, that other things do not, that living beings sooner or later die. We will try to take a similar approach to meaning: it may be hard to define, but we all experience it; we negotiate meanings in our daily life; we (mostly) know what we mean and what others mean.

In societies with well-developed literacy and a tradition of publishing and using dictionaries and other reference books, there is always a danger that a language will be equated with some written account of the language. We have already referred to the dangers of assuming that a dictionary of English *is* the vocabulary of English (2.2 above), and a book describing the grammar of English may likewise seem to *be* the grammar of English. But dictionaries and grammar books are only representations of the language (and limited representations of certain aspects of the language). If they have value, it is because they represent, in some generalizing abstract way, what people do linguistically. The meanings of words or the rules of grammar have not been laid down by some expert or authoritative decree at some point in the past and then enshrined in print. Dictionaries and grammar books are not legislation enacted by a linguistic parliament, nor are they the official manuals issued by people who created the language. If dictionaries and grammar books have authority, it is because they reflect general usage. Thus a language exists or lives not because it is described or recorded but because it is in use among people who know the language.

We say that people 'know' a language. And this, perhaps as well as images of language as recorded rules and inventories, may imply that language exists in the human mind. While it is obviously true that adult speakers of a language have large resources of knowledge – including, for example, knowledge of words and meanings and experience of using and understanding them – it would be misleading to suggest that an individual's linguistic knowledge is a complete and adequate version of 'the language'. For an individual, taken in isolation, is just that, an isolated individual. We cannot really speak of a language unless individual human beings are communicating with each other, bringing the language to life. Our individual knowledge of language comes from interaction with others, at first particularly with parents and family, later also with other children with whom we spend time, with schoolteachers, and so on. Some bases of our linguistic behaviour seem to be established relatively early and firmly. Most people acquire their accent or patterns of pronunciation fairly early and seem to change very little, even if they move to an area where people speak differently (although some people do make substantial changes in their pronunciation – for example, at secondary school or at university). People similarly tend to maintain basic vocabulary and idioms that they have used frequently in their early years, although again they may yield to strong pressures to change – for example, if they realize there are substantial social and economic advantages in making changes, or if they move to an area where some different words and idioms are customary. But even those whose language seems to change little during their lifetime are still using and experiencing language. For most of us, in most parts of the world, language is realized – actualized, made real – in a wide range of settings, such as homes and schools and workplaces and shops among many others. Our sense of what is normal usage, of what words mean, is constantly shaped by such experience. Consider, for example, the word *stakeholder*. Until the latter part of the twentieth century, the meaning of the word was something like 'the person who holds the stakes in a bet'. English-language dictionaries published before the 1980s record only that sense. By the end of the 1980s, however, the word was being used in a commercial sense, as in an Australian newspaper's reference to 'the best interests of the company taking into account the stakeholders'. From this kind of use in commercial and financial contexts, the word extended into other institutional uses, so that we find, during the 1990s, a university talking about its 'accountability and information provision to external stakeholders' and a water supply authority talking about workshops attended by 'stakeholders, managers and scientists'. A website relevant to the construction industry speaks of the importance of the 'collaborative efforts of all stakeholders' and then helpfully specifies stakeholders as designers, engineers, property consultants, technologists and clients 'among many others'. From uses such as these it is clear that *stakeholder* can no longer be taken in the sense of someone who is holding or directly investing money.

While it would be unwarranted to attach too much significance to a single word, the shift and extension of *stakeholder* illustrates not only how words and our understanding of them can change, but also how changes in words reflect social movements, in this case the widening scope of *stakeholder* going hand in hand with an increasingly commercialized perspective on services such as education and health through the 1990s and the extension of many commercial or financial terms into general administrative discourse.

The word *gender* has also shifted in recent years, again reflecting social changes. Until quite recently

English-language dictionaries gave as the main use of *gender* its meaning in grammar, as in talking about the two genders (masculine and feminine) of nouns in French or Spanish, or the three genders (masculine, feminine and neuter) of nouns in Latin or German. Some dictionaries also recorded a technical biological use of the word, as in talking about gender differentiation within a species, and an informal, possibly jocular or euphemistic use, as in talking about people 'of the opposite gender'.

By the end of the 1980s, dictionaries are recording *gender* as having a significant and formal use for something like 'the fact of being male or female'. The word has largely replaced *sex* in this sense, for *sex* has increasingly been used as shorthand for 'sexual intercourse'. At the same time, the word *gender* has increasingly appeared in various kinds of official and academic discourse. A corpus search suggests that in formal written discourse in the 1990s, references to grammatical gender were vastly outnumbered by the use of the word in phrases like 'redefining gender roles' or 'gender balance (in the workforce)' or 'gender and sexuality'. Thus demographers can refer to the 'age/gender profiles' of population groups and a trade union can raise the question of 'gender inequities in the existing staff structure', while universities offer courses with titles such as 'Gender and Policy' and the 'Politics of Culture and Gender'. Readers may like to ask themselves what they would take to be the current difference in meaning between 'the politics of gender' and 'the politics of sex'.

There is a sense in which the meaning of (most) words is constantly being negotiated. Our notion of what words like *stakeholder*, *gender* and *sex* mean is dependent on our discourse, on our experience of these words, on our experience of how others use these words in real situations. Older readers may remember uses that are now archaic or obsolete, like 'the gentle sex' and 'the second sex'. Even phrases that are current may reveal a certain competition between different senses: note, for instance, how we understand the word *sex* in 'sex discrimination' compared with 'safe sex', or 'sex stereotyping of women' compared with 'gratuitous sex scenes'. (Compare examples given earlier of meanings which may be associated with particular contexts, or of meanings which may disappear other than in a few phrases, such as *meat* in the sense of food in general, 2.3 above.)

The word *patron* comes from a Latin word that meant something like 'protector' or 'guardian'. In English, the word has had a similar meaning, still evident in the phrase 'patron saint', for example. When we read about the eighteenth-century lexicographer Samuel Johnson and his need for patrons (and see his biting definition of *patron*, 2.2 above), we also understand the word against a background of benefactors and their dependants. Current corpus evidence shows continuing use of *patron* in this kind of meaning ('galleries which were trustees of public art, with local government as their major patrons') but also shows the word with a meaning that is closer to *customer* or *client*, especially a customer in a hotel or restaurant ('most diners want privacy ... some patrons, however, do not mind being observed'). Meanwhile, the French word *patron* has come to be used in the sense of 'manager'. Thus in a restaurant in France, someone who asks for *le patron* is looking for 'the boss', not any of the customers. That two words of one origin can end up with contrasting, almost opposite meanings demonstrates again that meanings are negotiable and negotiated.

In the following section, we will further develop this perspective by looking briefly at the contribution to linguistic theory of the Swiss linguist Ferdinand de Saussure and the British linguist J. R. Firth. Saussure is widely considered to be the founder of modern structural linguistics and Firth a leading figure in mid-twentieth-century British linguistics. While these are by no means the only two linguists whose ideas we respect and draw on, they are both influential and explicit theoreticians who have shaped the way many linguists talk about meaning.

2.6 Saussure and Firth

Saussure

Ferdinand de Saussure was a francophone Swiss, born in Geneva in 1857. He seems to have had a great talent for languages and at the age of 15 was said to be already competent in Latin, Greek, German and English (as well as French, his mother tongue, of course). He came from a family with a tradition of scientific achievement – his father was a well-known naturalist, for example – and he entered the University of Geneva as a student of physics and chemistry in 1875. But his talents and enthusiasm were focused on language, and after a year of studying science in Geneva, he persuaded his parents to send him to Germany to study Indo-European languages.

Saussure studied in Germany for four years, mixing with learned and creative scholars, acquiring extremely useful experience in the research methodology of the times. He then taught for ten years in Paris, where he seems to have been highly regarded and influential, before returning, in 1891, to a professorship in Geneva. He taught mostly the linguistics of the time – Sanskrit, comparative and historical linguistics – but there is some evidence from his correspondence that he was dissatisfied with general linguistic thinking, that he thought there was need to reform the jargon and terminology of the day, and that he thought linguists needed to think more about what they were doing.

In 1906, the University of Geneva asked him to take over the responsibility for teaching general linguistics, and from then until 1911 he gave a series of lectures in alternate years. In 1912 he fell ill and he died in 1913. (For a concise account of Saussure's life and work, see Culler 1976.)

He had written a substantial amount about Indo-European languages and historical reconstruction, by which he had maintained his high reputation, but he had written nothing about his ideas on language in general. His colleagues and his students were so impressed by what they had heard from him that they thought they should try to preserve the lectures from the last years of his life. Two of his students put together what they could, from Saussure's own lecture notes and their and other students' notes, and created a book now known as Saussure's *Cours de Linguistique Générale* or *Course in General Linguistics*. The *Cours* was first published in Paris in 1916 and has been through several editions since then. A critical edition of the French text, prepared by Tullio de Mauro, was published in 1972 (Saussure 1972) and includes copious background and notes on the text. An English translation (by Wade Baskin) was published in 1960 and another (translated and annotated by Roy Harris) in 1983. Harris has also written a critical commentary on the text (Harris 1987).

Saussure is now famous for various points which are developed in the *Cours*. He made a clear distinction, for example, between describing the history of a language and describing how it is at any particular point in its history, a distinction between a historical (or diachronic) perspective on language and a current (or synchronic) perspective. If that distinction seems self-evident to us nowadays, that is partly because Saussure firmly established it.

Saussure devotes considerable attention to the nature of the linguistic sign, which he describes as an inseparable combination of a *signified*, a concept or meaning, and a *signifier*, the spoken or written form which conveys or represents that meaning. This view contrasts with a long and continuing tradition in philosophy and linguistics in which it is assumed or claimed that you can separate form and meaning. This difference of theoretical stance has many consequences – for example, for one's view of what translation is (see 2.10 below). We will therefore be returning to this point, but for the moment we note that Saussure says you can no more separate the signifier from the signified than you can separate the front and back of a sheet of paper.

Saussure's *Cours* also emphasizes the point that linguistic signs are arbitrary (although he elaborates and qualifies the point in ways that make a simple summary difficult). Arbitrariness is not just a matter of the lack of logical or natural connection – in most instances – between the meaning of a word or phrase and the spoken sounds or written form which represent that meaning. Arbitrariness is also evident when we compare languages and find that their signs and meanings do not neatly match each other. The Dutch *slak* could be either 'snail' or 'slug' when we translate it into English. English *blue* is two different colours in Russian. And in some Australian Aboriginal languages, what looks like the word for 'father' is a term referring not just to an individual but to a range of male persons, not only one's biological father but also brothers of one's father, parallel cousins of one's father and even certain great-grandsons.

Thus to speak of arbitrariness in language is not only to say that one concept in one language can become two in another, or that two can be collapsed into one. More than that, languages often see the world very differently. They divide reality up differently, they focus on different criteria, they structure experience in different ways. In the case of kinship-terms like 'father' and 'mother', English highlights biological relationships, whereas Australian Aboriginal languages focus on social structure in such a way that a word which English speakers might expect to refer to a unique individual refers rather to a group of people who share a similar place or role in the system.

In the kind of linguistics promoted by Saussure, it is important to do justice to the structures and systems which language itself generates or embodies. If you want to understand the kinship-terms of an Australian Aboriginal language, don't try to set up some universal transcendental framework, try to get inside the language itself. If there's a word that looks as though it means 'father' but evidently does not correspond with English *father*, the questions to ask are: what are the other kinship words in this language? How do they contrast in meaning with each other? How do they appear in discourse? What kind of systems and structures do they form or enter into?

These meanings may be arbitrary in the sense that there is no predetermined framework that says all languages must make this or that distinction, but they are certainly not arbitrary in the sense that individuals can play freely and randomly with the language. While there is of course scope for creative excursions, whether in the strikingly unusual turn of phrase of a poet or in the entertaining zaniness of a comedian, what holds a language together, what makes it work as a language, is the social convention or agreement that undergirds it. A word means what it means because that is what people here and now in this community take it to mean. At its heart, language rests on social convention.

For reasons such as these, Saussure is considered a modernist and sometimes compared with figures like Freud (born the year before Saussure) and Durkheim (the 'founder' of modern sociology, born the year after

Saussure). The three of them, among others, were leaders in a powerful movement that brought into the twentieth century new kinds of science and scholarship, behavioural and social sciences with their own thinking and methods.

Despite the fact that the Saussurean approach is not universally approved (see the following section for some brief comments on Chomsky's criticism of Saussure), it has shown its strength in its continuing appeal to substantial numbers of linguists and social scientists.

Firth

John Rupert Firth was born in England in 1890 and taught at the University of the Punjab from 1919 until 1928. Returning to England, he held posts in London, first at University College, then at the School of Oriental and African Studies, where he was the Professor of General Linguistics from 1944 to 1956. Much of Firth's work was in phonology, a field in which he was descriptively and theoretically innovative. (For introductory overviews of this work, see, for example, Robins 1979, pp. 214–21, or Sampson 1980, pp. 215–23.) But Firth also wrote about meaning and about language in general. Unlike many of his European contemporaries, Firth had extensive experience outside Europe. (In phonology, for example, he was alert to the dangers of assuming that a European alphabetic writing system was a good model of the organization of spoken language: while it is possible to draw an analogy between the letters of an alphabet and the phonemes or sounds of spoken language, there are significant differences as well as similarities.) Firth also read the work of anthropologists like Malinowski, whose charmingly entitled *Coral Gardens and their Magic* (1935) gave an account of the culture of the people of the Trobriand Islands, in what is now Papua New Guinea. Malinowksi stressed the importance of understanding language in its context and spoke of language as activity, explicitly rejecting the notion that language was a means of transferring thoughts or ideas from one person's head to another's.

For Firth, meaning is function in context, and, consistently with this broad claim, not only words but also grammatical structures and even the sounds of language have meaning. At times Firth seems to equate meaning with use (a word, for example, is meaningful because it serves some purpose in genuine contexts) or with context itself (a word's meaning is the range of contexts in which it occurs). While this has struck – and still strikes – many people as an unusual if not perverse extension of the notion of meaning, what is significant here is Firth's attention to what could be observed, and to genuine usage. Firth takes a theoretical stand not only against the kind of linguistic description which deals with invented examples considered outside any real context, but also against the kind of theoretical mentalism which presents speculations about the contents and workings of the human mind as if they were scientific observations.

The influence of Firth's views is evident in much of British linguistics: he was a major influence on Halliday, and hence in the development of modern systemic functional linguistics (see, for example, Sampson 1980, pp. 227ff., Martin 1992, p. 4, Eggins 1994, pp. 51–2), and on Sinclair and the development of corpus linguistics. The development of corpora – the large electronically accessible collections of textual material – has made Firth's seemingly bizarre statements about meaning as use and meaning as context far more believable. Now that it has become possible to track thousands of occurrences of words and phrases, in their real settings, linguists have begun to see just how informative a record of use in

context can be – and how wrong our intuitions sometimes are.

2.7 Cognitive linguistics

In contrast to Saussure and Firth, many linguists writing
in the latter part of the twentieth century have been
avowedly 'mentalist' or 'cognitivist'. The most famous of
these is Noam Chomsky.

Chomsky was born in Philadelphia in 1928. He
studied linguistics, mathematics and philosophy and
qualified for his doctorate at the University of Pennsyl-
vania, before taking up an academic post at the Massachusetts Institute of Technology, where he became
famous not only as a theoretical linguist but also as an
outspoken critic of the war waged by the USA in Vietnam
in the 1960s and 1970s, and as a writer and speaker on
US foreign policy, politics and the mass media. Encyc-
lopedias and dictionaries describe him variously as 'a
linguist, writer, and political activist', 'a political obser-
ver and critic' and 'one of the leading critics of American
foreign policy [since 1965]'. His published books include
not only widely read works on linguistics but also political works such as *Manufacturing Consent: the Political
Economy of the Mass Media* (with Edward S. Herman,
1988) and *Rethinking Camelot: JFK, the Vietnam War,
and US Political Culture* (1993). The titles of these works
already give some idea of Chomsky's stance: *American
Power and the New Mandarins* was dedicated to 'the
brave young men who refuse to serve in a criminal war';
and the phrase 'manufacturing consent' is often quoted
by critics of the modern 'free enterprise' mass media.

As with Saussure and Firth, it will be impossible to
do full justice here to an influential and widely discussed
scholar. (A brief but useful evaluation of the earlier years
of Chomsky's contribution to linguistics, psychology and

philosophy can be found in Lyons 1970; a later and more critical account is Chapter 6 of Sampson 1980; and Chomsky's more recent views can be found in Chomsky 2000.) Our concern here is with approaches to meaning, and in particular with twentieth-century mentalism and cognitivism, rather than with an overall assessment of Chomsky's work. And it is Chomsky's *Cartesian Linguistics* (1966) which offers us a classic defence of mentalism: the book is significantly subtitled 'a chapter in the history of rationalist thought' and it seeks to draw on and continue the work of the seventeeth-century philosopher Descartes.

In this view, there is a 'fundamental distinction between body and mind' (Chomsky 1966, p. 32) and the mind and its structure and processes are deemed to be a proper object of study. It is assumed 'that linguistic and mental processes are virtually identical, language providing the primary means for free expression of thought and feeling, as well as for the functioning of the creative imagination' (Chomsky 1966, p. 31). Thus the human mind has a certain structure and certain ways of operating, which in some sense determine – or even *are* – the structures and processes of language itself.

The programme of cognitive linguistics initiated by Chomsky and his colleagues in the 1950s and 1960s proposed a distinction between 'deep' and 'surface' structure in language. At least in the early stages of this programme, deep structure was assumed to have a mental reality closely related to meaning: 'It is the deep structure underlying the actual utterance, a structure that is purely mental, that conveys the semantic content of the sentence' (Chomsky 1966, p. 35). It was also suggested that this deep structure might be universal: 'The deep structure that expresses the meaning is common to all languages, so it is claimed, being a simple reflection of the forms of thought' (Chomsky 1966, p. 35). Those who followed Descartes 'characteristically assumed that mental processes are common to all normal humans and that languages may therefore differ in the manner of expression but not in the thoughts expressed' (Chomsky 1966, p. 96). This universalism is itself tied to the mentalism: 'The discovery of universal principles would provide a partial explanation for the facts of particular languages, in so far as these could be shown to be simply specific instances of the general features of language structure ... Beyond this, the universal features themselves might be explained on the basis of general assumptions about human mental processes or the contingencies of language use ...' (Chomsky 1966, p. 54).

As Chomsky himself sees it, his late-twentieth-century mentalist linguistics thus revives the concerns and perspectives of the rationalists of the seventeenth and eighteenth centuries and links them with modern psychology: 'it seems that after a long interruption, linguistics and cognitive psychology are now turning their attention to approaches to the study of language structure and mental processes which in part originated and in part were revitalized in the "century of genius" and which were fruitfully developed until well into the nineteenth century' (Chomsky 1966, p. 72).

Judged in this cognitivist light, the kind of linguistics which builds on the work of Saussure and Firth (2.6 above) is too sceptical about the mind and mental processes, and too oriented to what is observable 'on the surface'. In Chomsky's own words:

> From the standpoint of modern linguistic theory, this attempt to discover and characterize deep structure and to study the transformational rules that relate it to surface form ... indicates lack of respect for the 'real language' ... and lack of concern for 'linguistic fact'. Such criticism is based on a restriction of the domain of 'linguistic fact' to physically identifiable

subparts of actual utterances and their formally marked relations. Restricted in this way, linguistics studies the use of language for the expression of thought only incidentally, to the quite limited extent to which deep and surface structure coincide; in particular, it studies 'sound–meaning correspondences' only in so far as they are representable in terms of surface structure. From this limitation follows the general disparagement of Cartesian and earlier linguistics, which attempted to give a full account of deep structure even where it is not correlated in strict point-by-point fashion to observable features of speech.

(Chomsky 1966, p. 51)

This focus on mind and thought, backed by a dualistic perspective on mind and body, tends to assume that meanings are mental concepts which have real existence in the mind (as opposed to being convenient or theoretical abstractions or constructs). Previous sections of this chapter have already indicated that our view is somewhat different. Like the linguists whom Chomsky criticizes, we take it that the distinction of mind and body is an assumption, not a proven fact, and we are indeed sceptical about how much can be discerned within the mind. In fact the mind–body dichotomy represents a particular conception of humanity, a conception that is by no means self-evident and universal.

Firth was clear on this point: 'As we know so little about mind and as our study is essentially social I shall cease to respect the duality of mind and body, thought and word ...' (Firth 1957, p. 19). For Firth and many other linguists of the twentieth century (see Hasan 1987, esp. pp. 117ff., Halliday 1994b), the postulation of mental entities is not well justified and too easily takes linguistics away from its proper concerns with the physical, biological, social and semiotic character of language.

This section has given no more than a thumbnail sketch of some of the theorizing of Chomsky and cognitive linguists, and it is certainly not intended as a thorough review of this theorizing. Nevertheless, it serves no good purpose to avoid or disguise serious differences in theoretical stance which affect modern linguistics. We hope that some indication of the differences between Saussurean and cognitivist linguistics helps to clarify our approach as well as to remind readers that in linguistics, as in most human enquiry, there is no one theoretical position which is taken for granted by everyone.

2.8 Language and reality

It seems an obvious and necessary truth that language connects with reality, that language is in some sense grounded in reality. Words seem to refer to things that have an existence independent of human language, discourse somehow relates to actions and situations, language at large must be grounded in a world at large.

The fact that it seems self-evident to talk about a 'real world' to which language refers or relates actually has more to do with traditions and habits of talking and thinking than it does with objective necessity. It is customary to talk about words referring to things and about language connecting with reality; this does not mean that this is necessarily the best way of thinking about language and reality. We have already mentioned (2.2 above) the awkwardness of treating meaning as reference, of assuming that all words refer to things. For some words, it does seem quite reasonable to make a connection with a reality that is 'external' to language. But for many others, such a connection is speculative.

Part of being human is to try to make sense of the world and our place in it, and part of this endeavour is ordering and classifying the world, as we perceive and experience it. To a large extent, our language does the job for us. As children learn their first language, they learn categories and classes, usually without being at all conscious of it. We learn words for objects which we see and talk about, and these words imply categorization: a stick is different from a stone, a hill different from a mountain, a flower different from a fruit, a sheep different from a goat, a pen different from a pencil, a book different from a magazine, and so on. We learn words for colours, which give us a division of the colour spectrum, we learn words for human relationships, such as *aunt* and *cousin*, which bring with them ways of structuring our kinship, we learn verbs like *say, speak, stand, stay, steal, stumble,* among many others, which imply all kinds of distinctions and judgements relevant to human actions and behaviour.

It may be convenient for us to assume that this categorization is natural and universal. But this assumption will be constantly disturbed, as our experience becomes wide enough to realize that not all human beings live in the same environments, that there is more than one way of defining what flowers and fruits are, that some languages don't have a simple lexical distinction between hills and mountains or between sheep and goats, that some books look more like magazines and some magazines more like books, that communities have different ways of describing kinship, and so on.

Indeed, the more we widen our experience – for example, by learning new languages or by empirical scientific investigation of the nature of reality – the more we are forced to recognize that what we call 'reality' or 'the real world' is by no means as natural and self-explanatory as we sometimes like to believe. Consider, for example, the scientific discovery that colour is a spectrum, not a set of discrete colours, combined with the observation that different languages divide the spectrum differently. Descriptions like 'green' or 'blue' and properties like 'greenness' and 'blueness' cannot be considered part of an objective reality: they are at least as much due to the English language as they are to the 'physical' world. Or consider an example already mentioned in 2.6, the difference between the English word *father* and what looks like the equivalent word in some Australian Aboriginal languages: the Aboriginal word refers not just to the person we call *father*, but also to brothers of one's father, and even to male parallel cousins of one's father. There are many other related differences between the English and Aboriginal ways of seeing kinship. In general, the English terms highlight genetic relationships, while the Aboriginal terms focus on social structure. From the English-speaking point of view, my father and mother are individuals who are biologically or genetically related to me. From the Aboriginal point of view, my fathers and mothers are groups of people who are related to me communally or socially, by a structure of obligations and responsibilities.

At least as far back as Aristotle, human beings have also tried to describe their world more deliberately and self-consciously, in ways that might transcend or improve upon 'ordinary' language or 'naïve' thinking. Attempts like these underlie much of what we now call a scientific description of the world. We now have, for example, elaborate classifications of plants and animals that extend – and in some respects clash with – our everyday vocabulary. Thus most Australian speakers of English have a notion of what a 'pine' tree is, based largely on the nature of the foliage (evergreen needle-shaped leaves) and the overall appearance of the tree (with a relatively straight trunk and long branches bending out from it) and perhaps also on its smell and its sticky resin. The word *pine* is part of an informal classification of trees implied by the (Australian) English lexicon: pine trees are different from gum trees, wattle trees, palm trees, and so on. But in modern discourse we also have access to a far more elaborate classification of plants, the naming system sometimes called botanical nomenclature or the Linnean system (after the Swedish botanist usually credited with introducing the system in the 1750s, Carl von Linné, or in the Latinized version of his name, Carolus Linnaeus). In the Linnean system, pine trees belong to a genus known as *Pinus*, and particular kinds or 'species' of pine are identified in a standard way, by putting the name of the species after the genus, as in *Pinus radiata* (radiata pine) or *Pinus palustris* (longleaf pine).

Now, the 'scientific' way of naming plants is not simply a refinement of 'ordinary' vocabulary. For a start, the Linnean classification is based largely on observation of the stamens and pistils of plants, features which are significant in plant reproduction but not nearly as relevant in 'ordinary' discourse as the overall shape and appearance of a plant or its usefulness to humans. Partly for that very reason, there are trees which are not scientifically classified as *Pinus* species but which are nevertheless popularly known as pines – for example, the Huon pine (scientific name *Dacrydium franklinii*) and the Norfolk Island pine (scientific name *Araucaria heterophylla*). Similarly, there are 'gum' trees which do not belong to the *Eucalyptus* genus (such as the Sydney red gum, *Angophora costata*) and lilies which do not belong to the *Lilium* genus (such as the belladonna lily, *Amaryllis belladonna*).

Since the eighteenth century there has been an enormous expansion of taxonomies. The nomenclature of plants and animals are just two of the most widely known examples. Other fields in which classificatory naming systems have been developed include geology and mineralogy, anatomy (names of muscles, nerves, and so on), medicine (names of diseases, surgical procedures, and so on) and chemistry (names of chemical compounds). Indeed, many large industries have created their own nomenclature, such as an organized set of names for tools and procedures, or a systematic classification of products, components and spare parts.

Many of these taxonomies are supervised and regulated, by a company or an industry or by some international body like the International Union for Pure and Applied Chemistry, in ways that are unthinkable for everyday discourse. (Compare our earlier remarks on prescription and regulation in 2.4 above.) In the twentieth century, terminography or terminology processing (see e.g. Sager 1990, Pavel and Nolet 2002) became a field in which people could train and work. Terminologists may collect information on specialist terms, may provide information, whether in published glossaries or terminological databases or through an advisory service, and may provide advice and recommendations on terms and their use. They may be employed by companies and industries who maintain databanks of technical terms, or by publishers, or by bodies such as the European Union or the government of Canada who maintain large terminological resources particularly to support translation work. (If we include the many people working in non-English-speaking countries in agencies that coin and promote indigenous terminology, there must be far more people now employed in terminological work than in conventional lexicography.)

The classification enshrined in a taxonomy is (in theory at least) rigorous, and the naming conventions are precise and strict. For example, any species of plant can be placed within the 'Plant Kingdom' which is in turn divided into phyla, classes, orders, families, genera and species. The example below shows the classification of one species of pine tree mentioned earlier. The use of

Latinized forms ('Plantae', not 'plants', 'Coniferales', not 'conifers') is conventional and highlights the distinction between scientific description and everyday language. Note also the conventions governing the mention of a species: both genus name and species name are written in italics, the species name follows the genus, and the genus name takes an initial capital, while the species name is always given a lower-case initial letter.

Kingdom	Plantae (plants)
Phylum	Tracheophyta (plants with a vascular system)
Class	Pteropsida (plants with leaves with branched venation)
Order	Coniferales (trees and shrubs producing bare seeds, usually on cones)
Family	Pinaceae (trees with needle-shaped leaves, including firs, larches and spruces, as well as pines)
Genus	*Pinus* (pine trees, comprising about a hundred species)
Species	*Pinus radiata* (radiata pine, also known as insignis pine or Monterey pine)

Here are two more examples, first another plant, the musk rose (*Rosa moschata*), and then, from the animal kingdom, the silver gull, the common seagull of Australia (*Larus novaehollandiae*).

Kingdom	Plantae
Phylum	Tracheophyta
Class	Angiospermae (plants with their seeds enclosed in ovaries; flowering plants)
Order	Rosales (families of flowering plants incl. cherry, plum, strawberry, as well as roses)
Family	Rosaceae (flowering plants with typically five-petalled flowers)
Genus	*Rosa* (roses)
Species	*Rosa moschata* (musk rose)

Kingdom	Animalia (animals)
Phylum	Chordata (animals with vertebrae or a notochord)
Class	Aves (birds)
Order	Charadriiformes (families of gulls, puffins and waders such as curlews and plovers)
Family	Laridae (gulls and terns)

Genus	*Larus* (gulls)
Species	*Larus novaehollandiae* (silver gull, in Australia usually referred to as gull or seagull)

Conventions such as we have just mentioned – the use of italics, and so on – are by no means obvious. They can be enforced reasonably successfully, however, precisely because the nomenclature is used mostly in professional writing, subject to careful editing, as in scientific journals, technical reports and textbooks.

The discrepancies between such taxonomies and everyday language may be considerable. We have already mentioned pine trees which are not species of *Pinus*, gum trees which are not eucalypts and lilies which are not species of *Lilium*. In general, taxonomies serve to identify and classify large numbers of items: many of these items may be rarely, if ever, talked about by most people and the criteria by which they are classified in the taxonomy may also be marginal in daily discourse. Thus roses belong botanically in the genus *Rosa*, within the family *Rosaceae*. This family happens also to include blackberry and strawberry plants as well as the (often decorative and ornamental) herbs and shrubs of the genus *Spiraea*. But this scientifically established family of plants does not have any relevance in everyday discourse. Indeed, most people find it surprising that such a diverse group of plants should form one family. Similarly, it goes against habitual discourse to say that, botanically, a tomato is a fruit rather than a vegetable, or indeed that nuts are fruits.

This brings us back to the question of an objective description of reality. It is clear that nomenclatures of the kind developed for describing and classifying animals and plants and chemicals serve an important purpose: they are generally more comprehensive than everyday language, they are based on careful and often highly detailed observation, and they may bring with them valuable insights from empirical research. To that extent, a scientifically validated taxonomy may be closer to reality, or more revealing of reality, than everyday language.

Nevertheless, this does not justify the further step of claiming that everyday language is defective, misleading or in need of reform. In daily life, the categories of everyday language are likely to be more useful than a scientific nomenclature. The everyday English distinction between fruit and vegetables may not be entirely scientifically 'correct', but it is highly relevant to our eating habits and shopping practices. If I am planning meals and making up a shopping list, thinking perhaps about salads as light meals, or about cooked vegetables to accompany other food, or about desserts of fresh fruit, then it makes sense to think, as speakers of English habitually do, in terms of everyday categories. For my purposes, fruits do not include tomatoes or nuts, and it would be foolish and inefficient to suppose that they ought to. If I am asking a friend about fruit currently available at the market, or looking for fruit in a greengrocer's shop, or offering my guests a choice of fresh fruit to eat, none of us should feel any need to defer to a botanical classification based on careful investigation of plant reproductive systems.

Moreover, it should not be assumed that scientific taxonomies, once developed, reveal objective truth once and for all. The botanical and zoological nomenclatures, for example, are always open to revision and some areas of the taxonomies remain controversial. Sometimes a simple renaming has proved necessary: when the Australian platypus was first described scientifically, in 1799, it was given the species name *Platypus anatinus*; but it turned out that the term *Platypus* was already in use for a group of beetles, and a new genus name *Ornithorhynchus* was devised, so that the platypus is now described as *Ornithorhynchus anatinus*. Sometimes the taxonomy itself has had to be extended. Linnaeus and his

73

contemporaries in the eighteenth century probably believed that species of plants were invariant and invariable; subsequent research, including the development of evolutionary theory and empirical studies of diverse environments around the world, has led to a more flexible view. The plant taxonomy now includes subcategories (such as subspecies) as well as varieties within species. And sometimes, as a result of further research, a particular plant is relocated in the system — say, from variety to subspecies or from subspecies to species. (The example given above, of the place of the silver gull in the animal kingdom, should actually include a suborder Lari, below the order Charadriiformes and above the family Laridae, and a subfamily Larinae, below the family Laridae and above the genus *Larus*.)

The terms of a scientific taxonomy are in some ways more like a naming system than a vocabulary. In the Linnean plant nomenclature, for example, it is normal to refer to genus and plant 'names', and the typical genus species name, say *Pinus radiata*, is sometimes likened to a surname plus given name. Nomenclatures also tend to be recorded and explained in encyclopaedias and technical publications rather than in general-purpose dictionaries. Tendencies such as these inspire a tradition of distinguishing between encyclopaedic knowledge and linguistic knowledge, between 'knowledge of the world' and 'knowledge of language'. Thus, it may be argued, knowing the names of individual people, knowing historical facts and knowing about particular objects are all part of knowing about our world, and not part of our language. And it has to be said that there are things we know which are, on the face of it, quite outside language: telephone numbers, addresses, names of people and places, historical dates, and so on. Obviously, it is possible to be a fluent and competent speaker of English without knowing who the premier of Tasmania is, which is the largest city in California or when the kingdoms of England and Scotland began to be ruled by one and the same monarch.

But the line between factual knowledge and linguistic knowledge cannot be drawn sharply. We have referred earlier to the way in which names can become words (e.g. *boycott, sandwich,* 2.2 above). Some names of people and places – and 'facts' about them – are so well known in a community that users of the language do assume that everyone knows them. An old Australian idiom, *to do a Melba,* 'to keep saying goodbye, to make repeated farewells', drew on common knowledge of the singer Dame Nellie Melba and her several 'farewell' appearances. Legendary figures may figure in discourse as if they were common nouns, like King Canute, who is supposed to have commanded the tide to turn, unsuccessfully of course, but deliberately so, in order to demonstrate to his followers that there were limits to human power, even the power of a king. Thus a fiction writer says of a character that he was 'Canute controlling the waves' and assumes that readers will know the story of Canute so that they grasp the ironic meaning. In fact, the meaning of 'Canute' may have generalized to anyone who resists or denies evidence – or even to the act of resistance itself, as in the phrase 'doing a Canute'. On 24 July 2002, the Melbourne *Age* had a headline in its business section 'Bush does a Canute with falling US stockmarkets'. The article reported President George W. Bush's claim that the future was 'going to be bright', despite, in the words of the article, 'much evidence to the contrary'.

It may not be essential to one's ability to speak English to know who the first president of the USA was or who the prime minister of England was in 1945. But discourse does sometimes assume such knowledge in its meaningful progress. Some historical figures do carry meaning. An American writer refers to 'George Washington's cherry tree': according to the story, the young George chopped down a cherry tree and when questioned by his father, confessed to the misdeed, saying that he was unable to lie. The writer assumes that most or all readers will know the background story. Or, to take the example of the British wartime prime minister, a search of a few corpora for references to Churchill naturally produces many references to the man – in historical accounts, political discussions, and so on – but also yields some uses where the name is used descriptively, again presupposing that author and audience have some shared understanding or image of the man. For example, someone is described as 'of Churchillian mien'; a politician is recorded as having told reporters that a recent 'stirring' speech was 'his Churchill speech'.

In fact there is no way of drawing a principled distinction between knowledge of the language – the lexicogrammar – and extra-linguistic knowledge. Not long ago I was walking out of a particularly complicated car park in Canberra when a car pulled up beside me. The driver asked me if I could point him towards the exit – *any* exit – and added that he'd been driving round the car park for some time and had 'done more miles than Burke and Wills'. Now, I'm not sure whether I had ever heard that phrase before, and I don't recognize this as a familiar Australian idiom; but I do know (as probably most Australians do without having to look them up) that Burke and Wills were explorers who undertook an ambitious journey across Australia from south to north and then back again, but died of starvation before completing their expedition. Presumably the man assumed I knew that much, to be able to share in his self-deprecating joke about arduous and fruitless travels across a car park. (The Bank of English corpus records a couple of idiomatic uses: 'She's seen more Australia than Burke and Wills' is similar to the phrase I heard, while 'Waugh and Healy [Australian cricketers] are as much an Aussie institution as Burke and Wills' at least implies that Burke and Wills are well known in Australia.)

An example like this illustrates the uncertain edges of social discourse. Perhaps the man who spoke to me came from an area of Australia where his turn of phrase was a familiar idiom to most people. I might have simply been ignorant of his usage, just as any of us can easily find ourselves out of our depth when we move into a community where we are not accustomed to local usage. Perhaps he was simply an individual with a liking for a certain kind of Aussie imagery, and I will never hear the phrase again. Perhaps the phrase is in fact more widely used than I realize, and it's just that I have failed to come across it. Perhaps even my mention of it in this book might cause it to be quoted more often. Whatever the possibilities might be, the eventual status and meaning of the wording will depend on further usage, on uses which bring the phrase into play as an increasingly well-known idiom, or on absence of use which will ensure that the phrase does not enter a pool of linguistic resources or find its way into dictionaries and phrase books.

For words are first and foremost elements of text, elements occurring in actual discourse, not isolated items listed in a dictionary (2.2 above). Traditional lexicographers have separated linguistic knowledge from encyclopaedic knowledge by a process of decontextualization, trying to describe the meaning of words in isolation from their contexts. In this view, if we could detach from a word all its links to relevant contexts, we should be left with the isolated unadulterated meaning. But access to modern corpora has made it possible to study texts far more intensively, and corpus linguists are now able to show the semantic cohesion of textual segments. If we are no longer limited to single words detached from their contexts, if we do away with decontextualization, we need not insist on the distinction between linguistic and encyclopaedic knowledge.

What we normally call encyclopaedic knowledge is in fact almost always discourse knowledge. For most of us nowadays, everything we know and are able to know about King Canute, George Washington, the explorers Burke and Wills, and Winston Churchill, is based on texts. Even photos and film and video mean relatively little without accompanying text. If we consider how much our encyclopaedic knowledge owes to our discourse knowledge, the distinction virtually disappears.

2.9 Language and languages

The diversity of human languages is an inescapable truth. Some languages, such as those of Western Europe or the group of languages sometimes called the 'dialects' of Chinese, do show similarities, because of common ancestry or a history of contact, but many languages are strikingly different from each other. Even where languages have much in common – as English and German do, two languages which are historically related and which show many cultural similarities, including a long tradition of being influenced by Latin and French – differences are still of some consequence. Modern English and German are not mutually intelligible and it takes considerable time and effort for adult speakers of the one language to learn to function reasonably well in the other.

Taking a wider sweep across the world, languages differ more radically than English and German do. Phonetically, some languages have sounds and patterns of pronunciation which seem quite impossible to speakers of other languages. The click sounds of some languages of southern Africa seem odd and difficult to those who have not grown up speaking such a language; needless to say, there is nothing difficult or bizarre about these sounds to those who do habitually use them. The dental fricative consonant at the beginning of English words like *thin* and *thorn* is a constant challenge to those whose mother tongues do not have the consonant, while the various uvular and glottal consonants of Arabic strike a speaker of English as impossible to pronounce.

Grammatically, the patterns of one's own language become so habitual that alternatives seem perverse and sometimes beyond learning. Hence we hear people who have learned English as a second language saying things like 'you like coffee, isn't it?' (instead of 'you like coffee, don't you?') or 'I'm working here since 1995' (instead of 'I've been working here since 1995'). In so doing, they are simply following the patterns of another language and failing to follow those of English. And of course speakers of English learning other languages make other – but comparable – errors. The patterns of one's own language are 'natural', ingrained enough to interfere systematically with the learning of different patterns.

What is true of pronunciation and grammar is also true of meaning. Even related words which look or sound similar often differ in meaning. An example is a word already referred to more than once in this chapter (2.2 and 2.5), namely *patron*. Commonly used in English to refer to the customers in a hotel or restaurant, the seemingly equivalent word in French means 'boss' rather than 'customer'. Other deceptive differences between French and English include French *large*, which corresponds to English 'broad' or 'wide' rather than to 'large', and French *sensible*, which is closer to the meaning of English 'sensitive' than to 'sensible'. In French, 'sensitive skin' is *peau sensible*, and a sensitive or tender spot might be described as *l'endroit sensible*. But note how the words and meanings of different languages do not line up as perfect equivalents across languages: when the

French *endroit sensible* is used metaphorically it is probably better translated into English as 'sore point' rather than 'sensitive spot'.

To take an example from Dutch, the word *serieus* looks and sounds to an English speaker as though it ought to correspond to English 'serious'. And in a sense it does, in some contexts, particularly where a contrast is implied with humorousness or lightheartedness, as in a person looking a bit serious or a happy occasion turning out to be too serious. But this word is not used of, for example, a 'serious problem' or 'serious illness'. Here the relevant Dutch word is *ernstig*. You might shrug off a minor injury as *niet ernstig*, 'not serious', or you might be accused of *(iets) niet ernstig nemen*, 'not taking (something) seriously'.

More seriously, whole areas of meaning are differentiated and elaborated in some languages but seemingly unimportant in others. Some languages, like Dutch and Italian, have morphological devices for expressing diminutives which are used to signal not only the smaller size of an object but also (sometimes) endearment and informality. Compare Dutch *kast* 'cupboard, wardrobe', *kastje* 'little cupboard, locker', *kop* 'mug', *kopje* 'cup', *hand* 'hand', *handje* 'little hand'. But these so-called diminutive forms may be used in various ways: for example *handje* may be used in talking about a young child's hands but it is also the appropriate form in the metaphorical 'lend a hand' with a job. The informal or casual effect of diminutives is also evident in a request like *mag ik een sigaretje van je?* 'may I (get) a cigarette from you?', where the diminutive form *sigaretje* of course does not indicate that the speaker is asking for a small cigarette but is rather a device to downplay the request (somewhat as an English speaker might ask, strictly inaccurately, to 'borrow' a cigarette, or might add the word 'just', as in 'could I just ask you ...'). Some languages have similarly extensive use of diminutives – Czech and Italian, for example – but while English does have some comparable morphology, as shown by *book* and *booklet* or *dog* and *doggie*, it is not nearly as widely used, nor used with the same elaboration of interpersonal meaning. A language like English has an infinitely expandable set of numerals and considerable resources for talking mathematically – ways of talking about addition and multiplication and solving equations, and so on. By contrast, Australian Aboriginal languages have relatively few terms for numerals and few comparable resources (although with the arrival of a more technologically oriented culture in Australia they have started to acquire such resources). And so one could go on, comparing the more elaborate semantics of Australian Aboriginal kinship and clan structure with the simpler resources of English, among many other possible examples.

Languages do influence each other semantically, and this is an important observation for two reasons. First, it underlines the point that languages differ from each other, for if they were not significantly different, there would be nothing significant for other languages to imitate or acquire. Second, it is a reminder that while differences are real enough, languages are not always separated by impenetrable boundaries or yawning chasms. Just as individuals can learn foreign languages, so cultures can acquire the characteristics of other cultures – although it must be said that they never seem to end up identical.

In Australian Aboriginal languages there is usually a verb which refers to hitting or striking with an implement, potentially hurting or even killing, as in clubbing or spearing an animal. (A different verb is used of hitting someone or something with a missile such as a stone.) In Aboriginal English, the word *kill* is now used regularly

81

not with the sense of causing to die or ending life, but with the sense of attacking or hitting or beating up. The history of languages is full of such semantic readjustments, often in conjunction with major cultural changes. When Christianity came to England in the seventh century, not only did Old English adopt Latin words already in Christian use (such as *maesse*, 'mass', from Latin *missa*, and *scrin*, 'shrine', from Latin *scrinium*) but Old English words took on new meanings. The Old English word for 'build' started to be used to mean 'edify', on the analogy of Latin *aedificare*, which already had the sense of 'build up' or 'edify' as well as 'build' in a more material sense. The Old English *halig*, 'holy', was probably derived from a word to do with health or well-being (compare modern English words like *hale* and *whole*) but it came to be used in a specifically Christian way. In fact in the Old English period, the plural of the word was used to translate the Biblical 'saints', i.e. 'the holy ones'. This usage survives in certain names such as 'Allhallows' (All Saints) and most notably 'Halloween' (Allhallows Eve), but, in another semantic adjustment, the word 'saint' (Old English *sanct*, from Latin *sanctus*) has now taken on the Christian sense of 'a holy one'.

Just as Latin has influenced English, so elsewhere languages which were in one way or another dominant or prestigious, like Arabic as the language of Islam, or English as the language of the British Empire, have left their mark on many other languages. Thus Arabic has influenced Malay (now Indonesian and Malaysian) and Urdu, and English has influenced many languages of sub-Saharan Africa.

When the Netherlands ruled what is now Indonesia as the Dutch East Indies, the Malay that was widely used in the area took over many words from Dutch, many of them still evident in modern Indonesian, from *rem* for the brakes of a vehicle to *bank* for the financial institution, from *dokter* for a medical doctor to *gang* for a lane or passageway. As English words extended their meaning in the Christianization of England, so Indonesian words acquired wider uses in the period of Dutch colonial rule, as illustrated by the word *pusat*, which refers to the navel or to the centre of a (more or less) circular pattern like a thumbprint, but now also has a far wider range of uses for abstract and institutional 'centres' such as 'centre of gravity' or 'language centre'. As always, the semantic patterns of language shift and adjust. To take another example, the Indonesian word *rumah*, 'house', now enters into a series of specialized combinations such as *rumah penatu*, 'laundry', and *rumah sakit*, 'hospital', (compare Dutch *washuis*, 'laundry', and *ziekenhuis*, 'hospital', based on the Dutch *huis*, 'house').

Given the evident diversity of human languages and cultures, and the ways in which they interact, often influencing each other and copying from each other, but never quite ending up the same, it makes sense to say that languages have their own semantic strengths, their own areas of richness and elaboration. It is this that often makes learning another language a rewarding experience, an experience which changes one's horizon and opens up new views of the world. And this may make it seem all the more surprising that anyone has ever entertained the notion of universal grammar or universal semantics. In fact there have been a number of attempts to generalize across languages, to find a kind of ideal model or to find something that could be said to underlie all human languages. An arrogant but not unknown way of denying or minimizing language differences is to focus on one or a few languages and to regard any language that is not similar to them as deviant or degraded. European respect for Latin has sometimes led to this kind of view, especially when accompanied by an imperialistic willingness to dismiss many non-European languages as not really fully-fledged languages. But there have also been more thoughtful and more scholarly attempts to define some kind of universal grammar or universal semantics. We have referred earlier (2.7) to Chomsky's postulation in the 1960s of a 'deep structure' that might be common to all languages. Chomsky looked back to those who had thought along similar lines — for example, the grammarians working at the convent of Port Royal in France in the seventeenth century, who theorized that the categories and structures of grammar could be related to universal logic or universal thinking.

Universalism, as a theoretical position on language, usually rests on one of two strategies. One is to postulate something which is actually not observable, like a set of 'universal concepts' or Chomsky's 'deep structure'. Universal concepts, for example, could exist only in human minds, or perhaps in some common human consciousness, if there is such a thing. We cannot observe and record what is in the human mind in the same way that we can observe and record human behaviour, in particular what people say or write. This is in itself no objection to universalism as a belief, since most of us have beliefs of one kind or another, whether belief in God or in fellow humans or in ghosts or in good or bad luck, or beliefs about the future, or about what is valuable and significant in human living. But it is important to recognize the role and nature of belief here. Those who do believe in universal concepts underlying the semantics of all languages will argue that one can only put forward theoretical postulates and then check their explanatory power or test them against the evidence — for example, by looking for their consequences in observable behaviour. It then becomes necessary to face questions about what exactly constitutes a valid check or test of one's theoretical position, and not simply to begin to take theoretical hypotheses as probable or self-evident. Of course one can live by faith – as we all do to a greater or lesser extent – but faith needs to be acknowledged as faith, not presented as indisputable scientific finding.

The other strategy found in universalism is, in one way or another, to set up a supposedly universal framework or inventory from which all languages make some kind of selection. Thus one might claim that there is a vast inventory of universal concepts or components of meaning, including presumably very general ones like 'human' and 'animate' and 'concrete' (which might be semantic components of many words in many languages) as well as much more specific ones that would differentiate (semantically) a snail from a slug, a mountain from a hill, saying from telling, hitting with an implement from hitting with a missile, and so on. The fact that languages differ from each other semantically – for example, Dutch makes no lexical distinction between 'snail' and 'slug', just as English does not have separate lexical items for 'hit with an implement' and 'hit with a missile' – is then allowed for by saying that each language makes its own selection from the universal inventory. This is an interesting ploy. On the one hand it recognizes the difficulty of the universalist position, for the 'universal' inventory is no longer genuinely common to all languages. On the other hand it raises the question of what kind of existential status this inventory has. Since the inventory is by definition larger or more comprehensive than the semantics of any one language, it must exist beyond or above specific languages. If it resides in human minds, then part of it is redundant or irrelevant to the language(s) known to any individual mind, which must surely put that part of it well beyond any kind of empirical verification. And if it is not confined within individual minds, where is it to be found and how can we access and study it?

Much has been written about languages and their

differences and similarities. What we have said here goes only some way towards justifying our reluctance to postulate universal grammar and universal concepts and our preference for a more cautiously descriptive approach to linguistic behaviour. We emphasize again that we are not suggesting that languages are so different from each other that they constitute totally different worlds, cut off from each other. We do acknowledge that languages show similarities. But except where languages happen to be quite closely related, their similarities cannot be grounded in a core vocabulary or an underlying and invariant set of concepts or anything as temptingly concrete or specific as that. Rather, the similarities are better understood in terms of functions and general design rather than in terms of inventories of items or components or rules.

The analytical and theoretical problem here is not unique to linguistics or semantics, for it affects most of our study and understanding of humans and their behaviour and institutions. It is rather as if we set out to see what was common to wedding ceremonies around the world; or what was universal about food and eating; or what was common to all the world's practices of religious worship. We might try to find the objects common to weddings (such as rings or flowers or special clothing) or we might look for a universal underlying structure (for example, with people arriving, participating and departing in a certain typical sequence). But if we really pursued such a project along these lines, we would soon find it futile. Rings and bouquets and wedding cakes are indeed part of many weddings in many countries but they are not universal. They were certainly not part of most marriage ceremonies in Australia or Papua New Guinea or the Amazon Basin before the arrival of white colonists and their culture. In fact, the very notion of 'wedding ceremony' already suggests a European perspective on the event. If we wanted to assess universality in a more open-minded and realistic way, we would do better to step back from our immediate experience of weddings and to start to think in a more broadly functional way: how human beings form alliances or partnerships for sexual intercourse and parenting, how these partnerships are integrated into wider social structures, whether and how these partnerships need to be endorsed or recognized by other members of the larger society, and how these partnerships are entered into and characterized, in theory or in practice, by commitment and loyalty. Even here, we are still talking in English, using modern English words like *parenting* and *partnership*, which already project a certain light on what we think we are looking for and talking about. But at least at this point we have lifted our sights above a mere search for shared objects and entities, a search which is bound to fail, and we have started to think in a more general and productive way about what it is that characterizes people and their social behaviour as human. The wording used here may not satisfy everyone – I can think of several lines of objection to the phrase 'partnerships for sexual intercourse and parenting' – but if it is hard even to frame what we are studying, that is precisely because we are facing the genuinely rich complexity and diversity of humankind.

Much the same could be said about food and eating, or about religious worship. There are few, if any, foodstuffs which are truly universal. Even if certain items such as sandwiches and hamburgers are now obtainable in some kinds of hotels and restaurants around the world, they are definitely not consumed by everyone everywhere. Even items that are very widespread – say, bread – take different forms and shapes and are eaten in different ways. (Indian bread typically has a different appearance and function from French bread, for example.) What might be universal is rather the human need to eat, the need for substances such as starch and sugar, human enjoyment of eating, and so on. Likewise with the practice of worship in settings as diverse as the mosque, the synagogue, the temple, the church and the chapel: universals are found not in the objects and components that are present in worship but in the ways in which humans function as worshipping beings.

So also with language. If there are universals of language, they are best approached from the perspective of how language functions in human life and how it serves human purposes. All languages seem to be systems for making meanings, meanings encoded in wording which is expressed in spoken form (or, in the case of many languages, spoken and written form). All languages seem to provide ways of talking about things or entities and, by contrast, ways of talking about events or processes or relationships. (This distinction is often related to the grammatical distinction between nouns and verbs, but the relationship is by no means a direct and simple one.) All languages seem to project both experiential or representational meanings (relating to what can be said about the world and facts and events, and so on) and what can be called interpersonal meanings (relating to how speakers or writers are interacting with hearers or readers). This is a quite different approach to universals from one which seeks to find a common core vocabulary or a universal set of concepts. (For more detailed exposition of this kind of functional perspective on language, see Eggins 1994, esp. chapter 1, or Halliday 1994a, esp. pp. xvii–xx, xxvi–xxxv.)

2.10 Translation

Translation from one language to another is sometimes described as if it were a process of rewording the same meaning, a process of finding new words to express the same meaning. While this may sometimes be a convenient way of describing the process, and good translators do have a commitment to what we might call loyalty to the original, there are several objections to conceptualizing translation as if it were a process of taking meaning out of the words of one language and re-expressing it, unchanged, in the words of another language.

In the first place, most translators know from experience the rashness of claiming that they are preserving meaning unchanged. As we have seen in the previous section of this chapter, meaning is not isomorphic across languages. To take a simple example, if you translate the English word *sister* into the Australian Aboriginal language Pitjantjatjara, you have to choose between a word meaning 'older sister' and one meaning 'younger sibling'. (There is of course another Pitjantjatjara word meaning 'older brother', but there is no lexical distinction between 'younger sister' and 'younger brother'.) You cannot simply transfer 'the same meaning'. Information about the relative age of the sister may be implicit in the English text or may be entirely unmentioned and irretrievable. And even if you can establish that the sister is in fact a younger sister, you still won't be expressing exactly the same meaning in the relevant Pitjantjatjara word, since the sex of the sibling will now become as invisible as relative age is in English. Of course you can make a special effort to bring information to the fore, in both English and Pitjantjatjara: for example, in English it is perfectly possible to use expressions like 'older sister' or 'younger sibling', as we have just done above; but the words are still not exactly equivalent. English *sibling* is not a word which is normal in the English-speaking world in the same way as the Pitjantjatjara words in the Pitjantjatjara community. It belongs to anthropological or sociological discourse (or to discussions of translation!) rather than to talk of family and friends. I sometimes heard my father talk about his brother and sister, but never about his 'two siblings'; and I have sometimes heard my wife refer to her sister and (two) brothers but never to her 'three siblings'. In fact, even at this point, we have not exhausted the problem of translation, since the Pitjantjatjara words actually refer not only to brothers and sisters but also to parallel cousins (children of mother's sisters and children of father's brothers). But enough has been said to indicate that even apparently simple words cannot be assumed to match each other across languages.

This example has been a little too abstract. In real translation work, one has a context and purpose (say, translating a service manual or interpreting in a court of law or assisting in a land claim) and problems have to be solved in their context. Let's take another example and place it in context. Suppose I want to send a letter to a number of people around the world. Let's say it is a letter inviting them to contribute a paper to a journal. As I draft this letter in English I will have to make a decision on how to begin it. There are quite a few options. If I know all the names and can adapt each letter, I might begin each letter with a personal address, choosing among options like 'Dear Professor Jones' or 'Dear Susan' or 'Dear Sue'. If I am unable or unwilling to make each letter specific in that way, and am prepared to be rather formal, I can choose among options like 'Dear Colleague' and 'Dear Sir or Madam'. I can even take the option of omit- ting such an opening entirely. Without going through all the reasons why some people dislike letters beginning 'Dear Sir or Madam' and some dislike letters without any salutation at all, let us say that I opt to begin my letter 'Dear Colleague'.

Now I want to translate my letter, and I want it to be 'the same letter' in several languages. If I translate the letter into Dutch, I now have options which were not available in English. At the point where 'Dear' occurs in the English there are two possibilities in Dutch: *Beste*, which is appropriate for friends, and *Geachte* which is typical of official or business correspondence. (There is actually a third option, *Lieve*, but this is familiar and affectionate and not an option to consider in this context.) Thus there is no simple way to match the generality of English 'Dear ...', which can be used quite intimately ('Dear Susie') as well as very formally ('Dear Madam'). The Dutch version of the letter forces a choice between a more familiar option and a more formal one. Even in this small detail, we cannot claim that the Dutch letter will have exactly the same meaning as the English one.

In the second place, it is not at all clear that we have any way of separating meaning from wording. To hark back to Saussure's classic metaphor, a linguistic sign is like a sheet of paper, with 'thought' (or a concept or meaning) on one side and its expression (the form or actual word) on the other (2.6 above). One cannot isolate either side from the other (Saussure 1972, p. 157). What translators actually do when 'discovering' or 'analysing' the meaning of a text involves paraphrasing within the relevant languages rather than thinking in any genuine sense 'outside' the languages. Thus, when translators ponder what the text really means or search for the right words in the translation, they range over words of similar or contrasting meaning, over phrases that might expand the meaning or words that might condense the meaning, both in the language of the text in front of them and in the language into which they are translating. What they do not do, as far as we can understand the process, is to engage in some kind of abstract thinking that is independent of both languages. Consider the example we have just been through, of translating 'Dear Colleague' into Dutch. The translator, aware of the context, runs through options in both languages and thinks about what sort of equivalence might be achieved. It seems highly unlikely that translators engage in any sort of higher level abstraction in which they categorize kinds of 'dearness' (whatever that might be) independently of both Dutch and English.

Third, suppose that we could somehow separate meaning from wording. How could we then express meaning, other than through language itself? The suggestion that we can extract a meaning from the words of one language and then put it into the words of another, poses the question of where this meaning is and how it is represented when it is, so to speak, in between the two languages. In some cases, depending on the kind of text they are translating and its meaning, translators may be able to visualize objects and situations that are referred to, but even here it is doubtful whether they do this in a way that is independent of language. Is it really desirable, let alone possible, for a translator to imagine an agricultural tractor or a fluorescent lamp or a voicemail system without thinking of descriptions of it in language?

The examples that we have considered should make it clear that scepticism about metaphors of 'extracting' and 'transferring' or 'rewording' meaning is not the same as saying that translation is impossible. Experienced translators work quickly and skilfully with their linguistic material but they do not deceive themselves that they handle meaning detached from texts, nor do they claim to translate in such a way that their output is a perfect semantic match of the original text.

As Haas puts it:

> The translator ... constructs freely. [A translator] is not changing vehicles or clothing. [A translator] is not transferring wine from one bottle to another. Language is no receptacle, and there is nothing to

transfer. To produce a likeness is to follow a model's lines. The language [the translator] works in is the translator's clay.

(1962, p. 228).

3 The future of
lexicology

M. A. K. Halliday

3.1   Recent developments in lexicology

Towards the end of the twentieth century, significant changes were taking place in the theory and practice of lexicology, largely brought about by the new technology available for data-processing and text-based research. The two critical resources here are the computer and the corpus. Existing lexicographical techniques have of course been computerized. For example, lexicographers can now check their list of dictionary entries against other lists of words – say, a list of words occurring in recent editions of a newspaper – and can run such a check electronically in a fraction of the time that it would take to do this manually. But the computer does much more than speed the processes up – it shifts the boundaries of what is possible. For example, the total content of the 1989 edition of the *OED* is now available on compact disc (CD) to anyone whose computer has a CD drive. It thus becomes a database such that lexical information of all kinds can be retrieved from its half-million entries, with the entire search under any chosen heading usually taking less than one minute.

At the same time, lexical research can now be based on very large corpora of written and spoken language. Corpus work in English originated in the late 1950s, with the Survey of English Usage at the University of London and the Brown University Corpus in Providence, Rhode Island. The two universities each compiled a corpus of one million words of written text, in selected passages each five thousand words long. By the 1990s lexicographers could draw on massive resources such as the British National Corpus, the International Corpus of English, and the 'Bank of English' at the University of Birmingham in England; and indefinitely large quantities of text, from newspapers to transcripts of enquiries and parliamentary proceedings, began to be accessible in machine-readable form.

The effect of these resources on dictionary-making is already apparent: the dictionary can now be founded on authentic usage in writing and speech. This means that, in an innovative corpus-based venture such as the Collins COBUILD series of English dictionaries, not only is every citation taken from real-life discourse, but the way the different meanings of a word are described and classified can be worked out afresh from the beginning (instead of relying on previous dictionary practice) by inspecting how the word is actually used – what other words it collocates with, what semantic domains it is associated with, and so on. Here is an example of an entry from the first edition of the *Collins COBUILD English Language Dictionary*. The format of the entry has been changed slightly for presentation here, but the wording and sequence of information are exactly as in the 1987 edition of the dictionary. (A later edition of the dictionary has different wording.)

sturdy /stɜːdi[1] /, **sturdier**, **sturdiest**.
Someone who is **sturdy**
1.1 looks strong and is unlikely to be easily tired or injured.
e.g. *He is short and sturdy*...
...Barbara Burke, a sturdy blonde.
sturdily
e.g. *She was sturdily built.*
1.2 is very loyal to their friends, beliefs, and opinions, and is determined to keep to them, although it would sometimes be easier not to do so.
e.g. *With the help of sturdy friends like Robert Benchley he set about rebuilding his life.*
sturdily
e.g. *He replied sturdily that he had only followed her orders.*
2 Something that is **sturdy** looks strong and is unlikely to be easily damaged or knocked over.
e.g. *... sturdy oak tables...*
...a sturdy branch.

In the *Collins COBUILD English Language Dictionary*, an 'extra column', beside the entry, adds the information that *sturdy* is a qualitative adjective, in all its senses; and that, in sense 1.2, it is usually used attributively – that is, before the noun – as in *sturdy friends*. (This pattern is clearer in an example such as *they are sturdy supporters of the club*, where *sturdy* goes with the verb *support* (= *they support the club sturdily*). If the adjective is used predicatively – that is, after the noun – the sense will typically shift to 1.1: *the club's supporters are sturdy* = 'strong robust people'.)

The extra column also gives, in sense 1.1, the synonym *robust*; in sense 1.2, the synonym *steadfast* and superordinate *dependable*; and in sense 2, the synonym *tough*. This entry may be contrasted with the more traditional entry in another dictionary of approximately the same size, the 1979 *Collins Dictionary of the English Language*. (Again, the presentation here has been slightly changed, with more generous spacing than is normally possible in a large dictionary; and there are later Collins dictionaries than this edition.)

> **sturdy** ('stɜːdi) *adj.* -**di-er**, -**di-est**.
> **1.** healthy, strong, and vigorous.
> **2.** strongly built; stalwart.
> [C13 (in the sense: rash, harsh): from Old French *estordi* dazed, from *estordir* to stun, perhaps ultimately related to Latin *turdus* a thrush (taken as representing drunkenness)]
> − '**stur-di-ly** *adv.*
> − '**stur-di-ness** *n.*

We said at the beginning that lexicology − the study of words − is one part of the study of the forms of a language, its lexicogrammar. Lexicology developed as a distinct sub-discipline because vocabulary and grammar were described by different techniques. Vocabulary, as we have seen, was described by listing words, either topically (as a thesaurus) or indexically (as a dictionary), and adding glosses and definitions. Grammar was described by tabulating the various forms a word could take (as paradigms, e.g. the cases of a noun or the tenses of a verb) and then stating how these forms were arranged in sentences (as constructions, or structures in modern terminology). But vocabulary and grammar are not two separate components of a language. Let us borrow the everyday term wording, which includes both vocabulary and grammar in a single unified concept.

When we speak or write, we produce wordings; and we do this, as we suggested in 1.1 above, by making an ongoing series of choices. Usually, of course, we 'choose' quite unconsciously, although we can also bring conscious planning into our discourse. We also noted that some of these choices are between two or three alternatives of a very general kind, like positive versus negative (e.g. *it is / it isn't*; *do it / don't do it*); likewise singular versus plural number, first / second / third person, past / present / future tense, and so on. These 'closed systems' are what we call grammar. Of course, such choices have to be expressed in the wording, and sometimes we have specifically grammatical words to express them ('function words') like *the* and *of* and *if*. But often these general choices are expressed in a number of different ways, some of them quite subtle and indirect; so we tend to label them as categories rather than name the words or parts of words that express them. For example, we refer to the category 'definite' rather than to the word *the*, because (1) *the* is not in fact always definite, and (2) there are other ways of expressing definiteness besides the word *the*.

Other choices that we make when we use language are choices among more specific items, the 'content words' that we referred to at the beginning. These are not organized in closed systems; they form open sets, and they contrast with each other along different lines. For example, the word *cow* is in contrast (1) with *horse*, *sheep* and other domestic animals; (2) with *bull*; (3) with *calf* and some more specific terms like *heifer*; (4) with *beef*, and so on. So we refer to it by itself; we talk about 'the word *cow*', and define it in a dictionary or locate it taxonomically in a thesaurus.

We could describe *cow* using the techniques devised for dealing with grammar. We could identify various systems, e.g. 'bovine / equine / ovine', 'female / male', 'mature / immature', 'living organism / carcass', and treat *cow* as the conjunct realization of 'bovine + female + mature + living'. In this way we would be building the dictionary out of the grammar, so to speak. This may be useful in certain contexts, especially when different languages have to be interfaced, as in machine translation – different languages lump different features together, so their words don't exactly correspond. Equally, we could build the grammar out of the dictionary, treating grammatical categories as generalizations about the words that express them: instead of the category of 'definite' we could describe the various meanings and uses of the word *the*. Again there are contexts in which this might be helpful: teaching foreign learners who want only to read English, not to speak or write it, for example.

In general, however, each technique gets less efficient as you approach the other pole: you have to do more and more work and you achieve less and less by doing it (as we put it in our initial summary on p. 4, there are diminishing returns in both cases). What is important is to gain an overall perspective on lexicogrammar as a unified field – a continuum between two poles requiring different but complementary strategies for researching and describing the facts. This perspective is essential when we come to deal with the regions of the language that lie around the middle of the continuum, like conjunctions, prepositions and many classes of adverb (temporal, modal, etc.) in English. But it is important also in a more general sense. With our modern resources for investigating language by computer, namely 'natural language processing' (text generation and parsing) and corpus studies, we can construct lexicogrammatical databases which combine the reliability of a large-scale body of authentic text data with the theoretical strengths of both the lexicologist and the grammarian. The user can then explore from a variety of different angles.

One topic that has always been of interest to lexicologists is the recording of neologisms – 'new' words, not known to have occurred before. Earlier dictionary makers depended on written records, which are increasingly patchy as one goes back in time; the first occurrences cited for each word in the *OED* obviously cannot represent the full range of contemporary usage. The huge quantity of text that flows through today's computerised corpora (while still comprising only a fraction of what is being written, and a still smaller fraction of what is being spoken) makes it possible to monitor words occurring for the first time. But the concept of a 'neologism' is itself somewhat misleading, since it suggests that there is something special about a 'new word'. In fact a new word is no more remarkable than a new phrase or a new clause; new words are less common, for obvious reasons, but every language has resources for expanding its lexical stock, no matter how this is organized within the lexicogrammar as a whole. It is a mistake to think of discourse as 'old words in new sentences'. The chance of being 'new' clearly goes up with the size of the unit; but many sentences are repeated time and again, while on the other hand quite a number of the words we meet with every day were used for the first time within the past three generations.

3.2 Sources and resources

The best source of information about lexicology is the dictionary or thesaurus itself. It is important to become familiar with these works, which are now fairly common within the household. (In English-speaking countries at least, most large dictionaries and thesauruses are bought either for family members as Christmas gifts or for the children of the household to help them with their schoolwork.) You can consult dictionaries, to find out the meaning and usage of a particular word or phrase; and you can read them, dipping in at random or wherever your fancy takes you. They can be unexpectedly entertaining. As we have already noted in 2.2, Samuel Johnson's 1755 dictionary is famous for several entries that betray a certain personal perspective, such as:

> **excise**, a hateful tax levied upon commodities, and adjudged not by the common judges of property, but wretches hired by those to whom excise is paid.

Or you might come across a definition such as the following, from *Chambers Twentieth Century Dictionary*:

> **ranke**, *rangk, n.* (Shak., *As You Like It*, III.ii.) app. a jog-trot (perh. a misprint for **rack**(6)): otherwise explained as a repetition of the same rhyme like a file of so many butterwomen.

Nowadays dictionaries and other works of this kind are compiled for a wide range of different purposes. Naturally therefore they vary, both in the information they contain and in the way the information is presented. Consider, for example, an English–Chinese dictionary, one with English words listed and translated into Chinese. This might be compiled for Chinese students of English, or for English speakers studying Chinese; it might be for use in natural-language processing by computer (e.g. in multilingual text generation), or in the professional work of technical translators. It will be different in all these different cases. It soon becomes apparent that there is no single model that we can set up as the ideal form for a dictionary to take; nor are dictionaries totally distinct from other types of publication such as technical glossaries or travellers' phrasebooks.

This kind of indeterminacy is nothing new in the field. There is no clear line between a dictionary of a regional variety of a language (a dialect dictionary) and a dictionary of a functional variety of a language (a technical dictionary), or of a part of a language, such as a dictionary of slang, or of idioms, or of compounds. Nor is there any clear line between explaining the meaning of a word (dictionary definition) and explaining a literary allusion, or a historical or mythical event. The little dictionaries of hard words for children that used to be produced in various countries of Europe, like the Russian *azbukovniki* ('little alphabets'), included a great deal of useful information besides. In this respect they belong in the same tradition as *Brewer's Dictionary of Phrase and Fable* (first published in 1870, subtitled 'giving the Derivation, Source, or Origin of Common Phrases, Allusions, and Words that have a Tale to Tell') – and are only one or two removes from the great encyclopaedias of China and the encyclopaedic dictionaries of European countries referred to in 1.4 above. The line between a dictionary and an encyclopaedia has always been uncertain, and has been drawn differently at different times and places throughout the history of scholarship. Equally indeterminate is the line between a dictionary and a scholarly monograph: a dictionary may be conceived of purely as a work of linguistic research, like an etymological dictionary (typified by August Fick's *Comparative Dictionary of the Indo-European Languages* first published in 1868), or dictionaries of the elements that are found in personal or place names.

Finally, we might mention the comic dictionaries, like Douglas Adams' *The Meaning of Liff*, which consists of imaginary – and highly imaginative – definitions of place names treated as if they were English words. These in turn are part of the general tradition of lexical humour, which is found in some form or other in every language (the 'play on words' like punning by speakers of English). Related to this are various forms of word games, both traditional and codified: those in English include both competitive card or board games like Lexicon and Scrabble, and individual games such as plain and cryptic crosswords. In quite a few languages people play informal games in which they invert or swap syllables: rather as if in English we were to make *village* into *ageville* or *elbow* into *bowel*. And Indonesians sometimes create an 'explanation' for a word by pretending that its syllables are shortenings of other words; if we tried something comparable in English we might say that an 'expert' is someone who is 'EXpensive' and 'PERTurbing'. These games often fit a particular language – different patterns of phonological word structure lend themselves to different kinds of playful manipulation – but all of them provide insights into the way words work; and the special word games played with children, like 'I'm thinking of a word that rhymes with –', have an important developmental function in giving children a sense of what a word is, and how words are classified and defined.

Standard works written in English on lexicology include Chapman (1948), Hartmann (1983), Hartmann (1986), Householder and Saporta (1962), Landau (1989), McDavid *et al.* (1973) and Zgusta (1971). A more recent general introduction to the field is Jackson and Ze Amvela (1999). Green (1996) is a comprehensive history of lexicography, and Cowie (1990) is also a useful overview, from which much of the information in 1.5 above is drawn.

Glossary

affix
a meaningful element which is typically found attached to a stem or base; for example, in English the word *unwanted* contains two affixes, the prefix *un-* and the suffix *-ed*.

alignment
the process of aligning equivalent units in bilingual or multi-lingual **parallel corpora**, so that a unit in one language corresponds to the equivalent unit in another language and both of them can be accessed or displayed at the same time.

annotation
corpus-external information added to a **corpus**, such as **tagging** or information identifying the origin and nature of the text.

antonymy
the relationship of oppositeness in meaning, as in English between the words *good* and *bad* or *buy* and *sell*.

cognate, cognate word
(1) a word related to one or more other words in the same language by derivation, as in English *thought* is a cognate of *think*.
(2) a word which shares a common ancestor with one or more other words, as with English *sleep*, Dutch *slaap* and German *Schlaf*, which are all considered to be descended from an ancestral Germanic form.

cognitive linguistics
a branch of linguistics or cognitive science which seeks to explain language in terms of mental processes or with reference to a mental reality underlying language.

collocate
a word repeatedly found in the close vicinity of a node word in

texts; for example, in English the words *partial, lunar, solar* are collocates of the word *eclipse.*

collocation
the habitual meaningful co-occurrence of two or more words (a node word and its **collocate** or **collocates**) in close proximity to each other; as a lexical relationship, **collocation** can be defined quantitatively as the degree to which the probability of a word *y* occurring in text is increased by the presence of another word *x*.

collocation profile
a computer-generated list of all the **collocates** of a node word in a **corpus**, usually listed in the order of their statistical significance of occurrence.

concordance
a list of lines of text containing a node word, nowadays generated by computer as the principal output of a search of a **corpus** showing the word in its contexts and thus representing a sum of its usage; see also **KWIC**.

connotation
the emotional or personal associations of a word, often contrasted with **denotation**.

content word
a word with a relatively clear meaning of its own, in contrast to a **function word**.

corpus
a collection of naturally occurring language texts in electronic form, often compiled according to specific design criteria and typically containing many millions of words.

denotation
the central or core meaning of a word, sometimes claimed to be the relationship between a word and the reality it refers to, and often contrasted with **connotation**.

discourse
the totality of verbal interactions and activities (spoken and

written) that have taken place and are taking place in a language community.

etymology
an account of the historical origin and development of a word.

fixed expression
a co-occurrence of two or more words which forms a unit of meaning.

function word
a word with a relatively general meaning serving to express functions such as grammatical relationships, as in English the words *for*, *to*, *the*, in contrast to a **content word**.

generative
(of a grammar or a finite set of formal rules) capable of generating an infinite set of grammatical sentences in a language.

hapax legomenon
a word or form found only once in a body of texts; for example, in a **corpus** or in the works of a single author.

hyponymy
the relationship of meaning between specific and general words; for example, in English *rose* is a hyponym of *flower*

idiom
a type of **fixed expression** in which the meaning cannot be deduced from the meanings or functions of the different parts of the expression, as with the English idiom *kick someone upstairs* meaning 'move someone to what seems to be a more important post but with the motive of removing them from their current post'.

KWIC (short for **key word in context**)
a computer-generated set of **concordance** lines in which the node word is in the centre of each line.

lemma
a form which represents different forms of a lexical entry in a dictionary, as with the English lemma *bring* representing *bring*, *brings*, *bringing* and *brought*.

lexical item
a word understood as a unit of meaning rather than as a written or spoken form.

lexicogrammar
the **lexicon** and grammar of a language, taken together as an integrated system.

lexicon
the vocabulary or word stock of a language, usually understood as a lexical system or as part of **lexicogrammar**.

lexicology
the study of the **lexicon**.

lexicography
the art and science of dictionary-making.

mentalism
the belief in the reality of the human mind and in the possibility and importance of systematically investigating its nature.

meronymy
the relationship of meaning between part and whole, as in English between the words *arm* and *body* or *sole* and *shoe*.

monitor corpus
a **corpus** which contains specimens of language taken from different times (and is ideally regularly updated) and which thus assists the study of language change.

morpheme
the smallest element of language which carries a meaning or function, including **affixes** such as *pre-* or *-ed* as well as irreducible words such as *want* or *white*.

neologism
a new word, form, construction or sense introduced into **discourse** and ultimately into the language.

opportunistic corpus
a **corpus** which makes use of existing and readily available resources, does not claim to be representative, and reflects the assumption that every corpus is inevitably imbalanced.

paradigm
a set of forms, usually grammatically conditioned, based on a single **lexical item**, as in English the set *chase, chasing, chased* or *want, wanting, wanted.*

parallel corpus
a **corpus** which contains equivalent and usually **aligned** texts in two or more languages; it is sometimes called a **translation corpus** but does not always include the original text as well as translations of it.

parsing
grammatical analysis of a text, usually with the principal aim of identifying elements as subjects, nouns, verbs, and so on.

part of speech = **word class**

qualia
the felt qualities associated with experiences, such as the feeling of a pain, or the hearing of a sound, which are expressed by specific words.

reference corpus
a **corpus** which aims to be balanced and to reflect the contemporary language.

semantics
the systematic study of meaning in language.

special corpus
a **corpus** built for a special research purpose.

synonymy
the relationship of identity (or more realistically of near identity) in meaning, as in English between *dentures* and *false teeth* or *often* and *frequently.*

tagging
attaching grammatical labels, usually indicating **word classes**, to words in a **corpus**, usually by automatic methods.

term
a word with a meaning that is relatively precise and independent of the context, often subject to some special

convention or regulation, as, for example, with technical terms defined by standards associations.

thesaurus
a reference work in which words are grouped by meaning rather than listed alphabetically.

translation corpus
a **corpus** which contains an original text and at least one translation of it into another language; see also **parallel corpus**.

word class
a small set of grammatical categories to which words can be allocated, varying from language to language but usually including such classes as noun, verb and adjective; also known as **part of speech**.

References

Adams, Douglas, 1983, *The Meaning of Liff*, Pan Books, London.

Biber, Douglas, Stig Johansson, Geoffrey Leech, Susan Conrad and Edward Finegan, 1999, *Longman Grammar of Spoken and Written English*, Pearson Education, Harlow, England.

Brewer's Dictionary of Phrase and Fable, 1999, Cassell, London (millennium edition, revised by Adrian Room, originally compiled by Ebenezer Cobham Brewer and published 1870).

Chambers's 20th Century Dictionary, 1983, edited by E. M. Kirkpatrick, Chambers, Edinburgh.

Chapman, R. W., 1948, *Lexicography*, Oxford University Press, London.

Chomsky, Noam, 1957, *Syntactic Structures*, HarperCollins Publishers, New York and Glasgow.

Chomsky, Noam, 1966, *Cartesian Linguistics: a Chapter in the History of Rationalist Thought*, Harper & Row, New York and London.

Chomsky, Noam, 1993, *Rethinking Camelot: JFK, the Vietnam War, and US Political Culture*, South End Press, Boston.

Chomsky, Noam, 2000, *New Horizons in the Study of Language and Mind*, Cambridge University Press, Cambridge, Massachusetts.

Chomsky, Noam and Edward S. Herman, 1988, *Manufacturing Consent: the Political Economy of the Mass Media*, Pantheon Books, New York.

Collins COBUILD English Language Dictionary, 1987, editor-in-chief John Sinclair, HarperCollins, London.

Collins Dictionary of the English Language, 1979, edited by Patrick Hanks, William Collins, Glasgow.

Cowie, A. P., 1990, Language as words: lexicography, in N. E. Collinge (ed.), *An Encyclopedia of Language*, Routledge, London and New York.

Culler, Jonathan, 1976, *Saussure*, Fontana Modern Masters, William Collins, Glasgow.

Dictionary of Caribbean English Usage, 1996, edited by Richard Allsopp, Oxford University Press, Oxford.

Dictionary of Jamaican English, 1980 (rev. edn), compiled by Frederic G. Cassidy and Robert Le Page, Cambridge University Press, Cambridge.

Dictionary of Lexicography, 1998, compiled by R. R. K. Hartmann and Gregory James, Routledge, London.

Eggins, Suzanne, 1994, *An Introduction to Systemic Functional Linguistics*, Pinter, London.

Firth, J. R., 1957, *Papers in Linguistics 1934–1951*, Longman, London.

Fodor, J. A., 1975, *The Language of Thought*, MIT Press, Cambridge, Massachusetts.

Fries, Charles C., 1940, *American English Grammar*, Appleton Century Crofts, New York.

Green, Jonathon, 1996, *Chasing the Sun: Dictionary Makers and the Dictionaries They Made*, Henry Holt and Company, New York.

Haas, W., 1962, The theory of translation, *Philosophy* 37: 208–28.

Halliday, M. A. K., 1994a (2nd edn), *An Introduction to Functional Grammar*, Edward Arnold, London.

Halliday, M. A. K., 1994b, On language in relation to the evolution of human consciousness, in S. Allen (ed.), *Of Thoughts and Words – Proceedings of Nobel Symposium 92: The Relation Between Language and Mind*, World Scientific Publishing, Singapore and London.

Harris, Roy, 1987, *Reading Saussure: a Critical Commentary on the Cours de Linguistique Générale*, Duckworth, London.

Hartmann, R. R. K., 1983, *Lexicography: Principles and Practice*, Academic Press, London and New York.

Hartmann, R. R. K., 1986, *The History of Lexicography*, John Benjamins, Amsterdam and Philadelphia.

Hartmann, R. R. K., 2001, *Teaching and Researching Lexicography*, Longman Pearson Education, Harlow.

Hasan, Ruqaiya, 1987, Directions from structuralism, in N. Fabb, D. Attridge, A. Durant and C. MacCabe (eds), *The Linguistics of Writing: Arguments Between Language and Literature*, Manchester University Press, Manchester.

Householder, Fred W. and Sol Saporta (eds), 1962, *Problems in Lexicography*, Indiana University Press, Bloomington.

Jackson, H. and E. Ze Amvela, 1999, *Word Meaning and Vocabulary: an Introduction to Modern English Lexicology*, Cassell, London.

Johnson's Dictionary: A Modern Selection by E. L. McAdam and George Milne, 1995, Cassell, London.

Landau, Sidney I., 1989 (2nd edn), *Dictionaries: the Art and Craft of Lexicography*, Cambridge University Press, Cambridge.

Larousse, Pierre, 1865–76, *Grand Dictionnaire Universel du XIXe Siècle*, 15 vols, Librairie Larousse, Paris. (Supplements published 1878, 1890 and various editions published later.)

Lewis, Charlton T. and Charles Short, 1879, *A Latin Dictionary: Founded on Andrews' Edition of Freund's Latin Dictionary, revised, enlarged and in great part rewritten by Charlton T. Lewis and Charles Short*, Oxford University Press, Oxford. (Various editions published later.)

Liddell, Henry George and Robert Scott, 1843, *Greek–English Lexicon*, Oxford University Press, Oxford. (Various editions published later.)

Littré, Emile, 1863–73, *Dictionnaire de la Langue Française* (Supplement published 1878 and various editions published later.)

Longman Dictionary of Contemporary English, 1978, editor-in-chief Paul Procter, Longman, London.

Longman Dictionary of Contemporary English, 1987 (new edn), editorial director Della Summers, Longman, Harlow.

Longman Dictionary of English Idioms, 1979, Longman, Harlow and London.

Lyons, J., 1970, *Chomsky*, Fontana Modern Masters, William Collins, London.

Lyons, J., 1977, *Semantics*, 2 vols, Cambridge University Press, Cambridge.

McArthur, Tom (ed.), 1992, *The Oxford Companion to the English Language*, Oxford University Press, Oxford.

McDavid Jr, Raven I. and Audrey R. Duckert (eds), 1973, *Lexicography in English*, New York Academy of Sciences, Annals 211, New York.

Macquarie Dictionary, 1997 (3rd edn), editor-in-chief Arthur Delbridge, Macquarie Library, Sydney.

Macquarie Concise Dictionary, 1998 (3rd edn), general editors A. Delbridge and J. R. L. Bernard, Macquarie Library, Sydney.

Malinowksi, B., 1935, *Coral Gardens and their Magic*, 2 vols, Allen & Unwin, London.

Martin, J. R., 1992, *English Text: System and Structure*, John Benjamins, Philadelphia and Amsterdam.

New English Dictionary on Historical Principles, 1884–1928, edited by James A. H. Murray, H. Bradley, W. A. Craigie and C. T. Onions, Clarendon Press, Oxford.

New Oxford Dictionary of English, 2001, Oxford University Press, Oxford.

New Shorter Oxford English Dictionary on Historical Principles, 1993 (rev. edn), 2 vols, edited by Lesley Brown, Clarendon Press, Oxford.

Oxford Dictionary of New Words, 1997, edited by E. Knowles and J. Elliott, Oxford University Press, Oxford.

Oxford English Dictionary, 1989 (revised edition of the *New English Dictionary on Historical Principles*), 20 vols, prepared by J. A. Simpson and E. S. C. Weiner, Clarendon Press, Oxford.

Pavel, Silvia, and Diane Nolet, 2002, *Handbook of Terminology*, Terminology and Standardization Translation Bureau, Ministry of Public Works and Government Services, Canada.

Quirk, R., S. Greenbaum, G. Leech and J. Svartvik, 1985, *A Comprehensive Grammar of the English Language*, Longman, London.

Robins, R. H., 1979 (2nd edn), *A Short History of Linguistics*, Longman, London.

Roget, Peter Mark, 1852, *Thesaurus of English Words and Phrases*, Longman, Brown, Green and Longman, London. (Various editions published later.)

Sager, Juan C., 1990, *A Practical Course in Terminology Processing*, John Benjamins, Amsterdam and Philadelphia.

Sampson, Geoffrey, 1980, *Schools of Linguistics: Competition and Evolution*, Hutchinson, London.

de Saussure, Ferdinand, 1960, *Course in General Linguistics*, Peter Owen, London (translated by Wade Baskin).

de Saussure, Ferdinand, 1972, *Cours de Linguistique Générale*, Editions Payot, Paris (édition critique préparée par Tullio de Mauro).

de Saussure, Ferdinand, 1983, *Course in General Linguistics*, Duckworth, London (translated by Roy Harris).

Sinclair, J. (ed.), 1987, *Looking Up: An Account of the Cobuild Project in Lexical Computing*, HarperCollins, London.

Sinclair, J., 1991, *Corpus, Collocation, Concordance*, Oxford University Press, Oxford.

Sinclair, J., 1996, 'The Empty Lexicon', *International Journal of Corpus Linguistics* 1: 99–119.

Strang, Barbara M. H., 1970, *A History of English*, Methuen, London.

Warburg, Jeremy, 1968, 'Notions of correctness, supplement to Quirk, Randolph (2nd edn), *The Use of English*', Longman, London and Harlow.

Webster, Noah, 1828, *American Dictionary of the English Language*.

Wright, Joseph, 1898–1905, *The English Dialect Dictionary, being the complete vocabulary of all dialect words still in use, or known to have been in use during the last two hundred years*, 6 vols, Henry Frowde, London.

Zgusta, Ladislaw, 1971, *Manual of Lexicography*, Mouton, The Hague.

Corpora

The Bank of English, http://titania@bham.ac.uk

British National Corpus, http://www.natcorp.ox.ac.uk/

Brown Corpus, manual available at http://icame.uib.no/brown/ bcm.html

International Corpus of English (ICE), http://www.ucl.ac.uk/ english-usage/ice/

London Lund Corpus, http://khnt.hit.uib.no/icame/manuals/LOND LUND/INDEX.HTM

Index

(words in bold can be found in the Glossary)